Chandragupta Maurya

Reconstructing Indian History & Culture
(ISSN 0971-3824)

1. Society in Ancient India; by Sures Chandra Banerji (ISBN 81-246-0000-7)
2. Political Thought in Ancient India; by G.P. Singh (ISBN 81-246-0001-5)
3. Early Indian Historical Tradition and Archaeology; by G.P. Singh (ISBN 81-246-0005-8)
4. Vasantotsava: The Spring Festivals of India; by Leona M. Anderson (ISBN 81-246-0011-2)
5. Ecological Readings in the Veda; by M. Vannucci (ISBN 81-246-0009-0)
6. Vṛndāvana in Vaiṣṇava Literature; by Maura Corcoran (ISBN 81-246-0024-4)
7. Social History of the Tamils (1707-1947); by P. Subramanian (ISBN 81-246-0045-7)
8. Ancient Indian Coinage; by Rekha Jain (ISBN 81-246-0051-1)
9. Buddhism and Socio-Economic Life of Eastern India; by Bimal Chandra Mohapatra (ISBN 81-246-0055-4)
10. Chandragupta Maurya; by P.L. Bhargava (ISBN 81-246-0056-2)
11. Mṛtyu: Concept of Death in Indian Traditions; by Gian Giuseppe Filippi (ISBN 81-246-0072-4)
12. Yama: The Glorious Lord of the Other World; by Kusum P. Merh (ISBN 81-246-0066-X)
13. Sacred Complex of Ujjain; by D.K. Samanta (ISBN 81-246-0078-3)
14. Vedic View of the Earth; by S.R.N. Murthy (ISBN 81-246-0091-0)
15. Society in the Atharvaveda; by B.S. Kharade (ISBN 81-246-0093-7)
16. Orissan History, Culture and Archaeology; by S. Pradhan (ISBN 81-246-0117-8)
17. Education in Ancient India; by Mitali Chatterjee (ISBN 81-246-0113-5)
18. Surā: The Liquor and the Vedic Sacrifice; by M.B. Kolhatkar (ISBN 81-246-0114-3)
19. Human Ecology in the Vedas; by Marta Vannucci (ISBN 81-246-0115-1)
20. Governance in Ancient India; by Anupa Chandra Pandey (ISBN 81-246-0135-6)
21. The Cultural Glory of Ancient India: A Literary Overview; by Sures Chandra Banerji (ISBN 81-246-0137-2)
22. Kauṭilya's Arthaśāstra in the light of Modern Science & Technology; by Sunil Sen Sarma (ISBN 81-246-0187-9)
23. History of Jainism — With Special Reference to Mathurā; by V.K. Sharma (ISBN 81-246-0195-X)
24. Cultural Tourism in India: Museums, Monuments & Arts — Theory and Practice; by S.P. Gupta; Krishna Lal; Mahua Bhattacharya (ISBN 81-246-0215-8)
25. Ancient Indian Historiography — Sources and Interpretations; by G.P. Singh (ISBN 81-246-0228-X)
26. Republics, Kingdoms, Towns and Cities in Ancient India; by G.P. Singh (ISBN 81-246-0237-9)
27. Facets of Ancient Indian History and Culture — New Perception; by G.P. Singh (ISBN 81-246-0238-7)
28. Kamakhya — A Socio-cultural Study; by Nihar Ranjan Mishra (ISBN 81-246-0251-4)
29. History and Culture of Tamil Nadu as Gleaned from the Sanskrit Inscriptions Vol. 1 (up to c. AD 1310); by Chithra Madhavan (ISBN 81-246-0308-1).
30. Life Style of the Vedic People; by Pranati Ghosal (ISBN 81-246-0344-8)
31. History and Culture of Tamil Nadu as Gleaned from the Sanskrit Inscriptions Vol. 2 (up to c. AD 1310 - c. 1885 AD); by Chithra Madhavan (ISBN 81-246-0380-4).

Reconstructing Indian History & Culture, no. 10

Chandragupta Maurya

A Gem of Indian History

Purushottam Lal Bhargava

D.K. Printworld (P) Ltd.
New Delhi

Cataloging in Publication Data — DK

Bhargava, Purushottam Lal, 1909-2002.
Chandragupta Maurya — a gem of Indian history.
(Reconstructing Indian history & culture; no. 10).
Includes bibliographical references (p.).
Includes index.
ISBN 8124600562

1. Chandragupta Maurya, *Emperor of Northern India*. 2. Maurya dynasty. 3. India — History — 324 BCE – CE 1000. I. Title. II. Series: Reconstructing Indian history & culture; no. 10.

ISBN 81-246-0056-2
Second Revised and Enlarged Edition, 1996
Second impression, 2007

Published and printed by:
D.K. Printworld (P) Ltd.
Regd. Office: 'Sri Kunj,' F-52, Bali Nagar
Ramesh Nagar Metro Station
New Delhi-110 015
Phones: (011) 2545 3975; 2546 6019; *Fax*: (011) 2546 5926
E-mail: dkprintworld@vsnl.net
Website: www.dkprintworld.com

To
the deeply cherished and evergreen memory of
my beloved brother
Sarvottam

वाराहीमात्मयोनेस्तनुमवनविधावास्थितस्यानुरूपां
यस्य प्राग्दन्तकोटिं प्रलयपरिगता शिश्रिये भूतधात्री।
म्लेच्छैरुद्विज्यमाना भुजयुगमधुना संश्रिता राजमूर्तेः
स श्रीमद्बन्धुभृत्यश्चिरमवतु महीं पार्थिवश्चन्द्रगुप्तः।।

— *Mudrārākṣasa*, VII, 19.

Preface
To The Second Edition

THE first edition of this book, which was published sixty years ago in 1935 when I had just finished my student career, received tremendous welcome both from eminent scholars of Indian history and prestigious journals. It was sold out in a very short period.

There has been a presistent demand for a second edition of this book. But due to my involvement in writing other books, besides my duties as a teacher of post-graduate classes and research guide, I could not get time to revise this book for a long period and so many decades passed away almost unnoticed.

At last I realized that the work could not be postponed any further. But as much water had flown down the river Ganga since the publication of the first edition of this book and much new material on the subject had seen the light of the day, I clearly perceived that many of the views expressed by me in the first edition needed modification and many things dealt with in an incipient manner in that edition needed a much more detailed treatment. In other words the book needed a complete and thorough revision. This was done by me and I am happy to place the new edition in the hands of readers.

My daughter Mira, my son Divakar and my grandson Manjul deserve the highest praise for typing and preparing a faultless manuscript. My granddaughter Mudita too gave me laudable and ungrudging help in correcting the proofs and preparing the initial index of this book. The two promising young scholars, Sanjay Jain and Adhyatm Jain deserve commendation and thanks for the hard work they did in giving final shape to the Index. Finally I must express my heartfelt thanks to the publishers of this book Messers D.K. Printworld (P) Ltd. who have done their job both nicely and expeditiously.

Jaipur
July 15, 1995

P. L. Bhargava

Preface
To The First Edition

As a student of history I have always been fascinated by the career of Chandragupta Maurya, one of the greatest of kings, conquerors and administrators the world has produced. In this small monograph I have tried to describe, in a brief compass, the life and career of Chandragupta making use of all the original sources I could lay my hands upon. I have deviated from the accepted views where I found better evidence to the contrary. For instance, I have accepted the Jain date for the coronation of Chandragupta as it is better supported by facts than the date hitherto generally accepted. In some matters, of course, it is difficult to achieve any kind of finality till further evidence comes to notice, for example in the case of the pre-Maurya history of Magadha; in such cases I have simply mentioned the probabilities without emphasising the correctness of my views.

Recently, there have been controversies on many points, of more or less important bearing on the subject. I have referred to them in the text where relevant, but I would like to mention one of them here as the text was already printed when it came to my notice. I refer to the controversy regarding the relation of the *Brihatkatha* to the *Mudrarakshasa*. Mr. C.D. Chatterji, in a very learned article, which appeared in the *Indian Culture*, Vol. I no. 2, has expressed doubt on the authenticity of the statement found in the *Dasarupavaloka* that the *Mudrarakshasa* was based on the *Brihatkatha*, and has shown at length that the two verses following in support of this statement are later interpolations. His arguments in support of the view that the plot of the *Mudrarakshasa* cannot have been taken from the *Brihatkatha* are, no doubt, convincing. Yet, there is nothing to disprove the probability that the idea of Chandragupta's Nanda descent was suggested to *Visakhadatta* by the *Brihatkatha*.

Unfortunately, the book suffers from the lack of proper diacritical marks for Sanskrit words as also from a few printing errors here and there. I hope to remedy them in the next edition.

These observations will be incomplete if I did not express my obligation to the different persons from whom I received inspiration and help. If it be not regarded as too personal I shall, among them, place first my dear father, who goaded me to write out these pages. Among those from whom I received constant encouragement, I would like to mention the names of my kind teacher Mr. K.A.S. Iyer, M.A., Head of the Sanskrit Department, Lucknow University, and Pandit Brijnath Sharga, M.A., LL.B., Advocate. Mr C.D. Chatterji, M.A., of the Lucknow University, for whom I entertain high regard as my teacher, was very kind to suggest to me some original sources for the work and to give me his ungrudging help whenever I approached him for the same. I am indebted to Dr. Rama Shanker Tripathi, M.A., Ph. D., of the Banares Hindu University, for suggesting to me certain papers which proved very useful in my work. I have reserved the expression of my gratitude to my esteemed teacher, Dr. Radha Kumud Mookerji, M.A., Ph. D., an authority on Ancient India, not because he deserves the least but because I cannot find adequate words for it. I feel infinite satisfaction when I see this humble attempt so well reviewed by such a high authority on the subject.

Lucknow
January 1, 1935

P. L. Bhargava

Contents

	Preface to the Second Edition	vii
	Preface to the First Edition	ix
	Map of India in 300 BCE	xiii
1.	Chronology and Sources	1
2.	Rise and Growth of the Kingdom of Magadha	15
3.	Career of Candragupta	33
4.	Administration of the Empire	49
5.	Religious, Social and Economic Conditions	71
6.	Literature and Art	99
7.	Achievements of Candragupta	113
8.	Legends of Candragupta	117
	Appendix	129
	Bibliography	133
	Index	141

Spelling of **Chandragupta Maurya** has been trans-literated as **Candragupta Maurya** throughout the text, whereas on cover and title-page the prevalent spelling has been used to avoid any confusion among users.

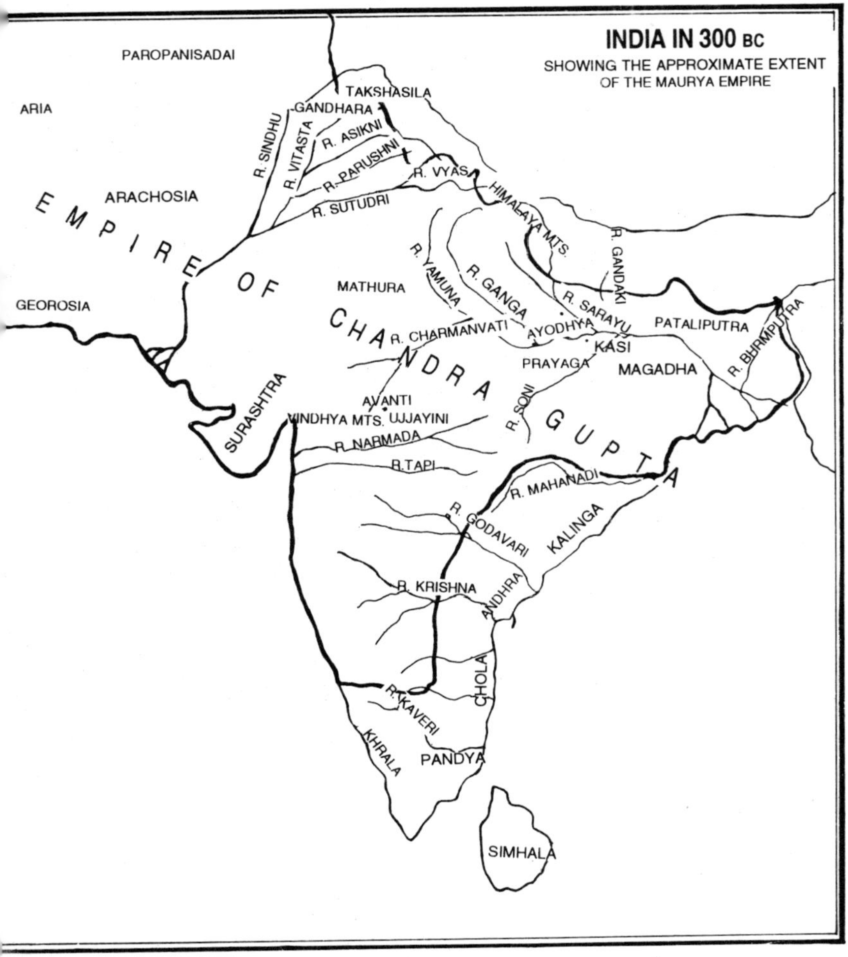

INDIA IN 300 BC

SHOWING THE APPROXIMATE EXTENT OF THE MAURYA EMPIRE

1

Chronology and Sources

Chronology

THANKS to Sir William Jones' identification of Sandrakottos, mentioned by classical writers as a contemporary of Alexander the Great, with Candragupta, the founder of the Maurya empire, the problem of ancient Indian chronology has become comparatively easy to solve.[1] Many other sources have since been discovered which are capable of rendering further valuable aid in this direction. The Purāṇic genealogies when read with the Buddhist chronicles of Sri Lanka and the Jain records go a long way in solving the vexed problem of chronology.

Buddhist and Jain authors base their calculations on the dates of the demise of Gautama Buddha and Mahāvīra respectively. The date of the *nirvāṇa* of Buddha has been a subject of keen controversy, and scholars have been vacillating between 544 BCE, the Sri Lankan date of the *Great Decease*, and 486 BCE, the starting point of the dotted record found at the Chinese city of Canton. There are, however, two important considerations which go in favour of the Sri Lankan date. In the first place, as observed by Max-Müller long ago, the process of adding one dot at the end of each year during so long a time as 975 years was extremely precarious. Secondly, the Cantonese date goes against the unanimous Buddhist and Jain tradition of the contemporaneity of Buddha and Mahāvīra. According to the Jain tradition, Mahāvīra attained liberation 470 years before the birth of Vikrama which took place 18 years before the foundation of the Vikrama era of 57 BCE. The traditional date of the passing away of Mahāvīra is thus 470+57+18 = 545 BCE.[2] The date of the birth of Buddha according to the Cantonese reckoning is 566 BCE and this would mean that Buddha was 21 years old when Mahāvīra died, whereas according to Buddhist canonical texts the former was a renowned religious teacher of long standing when the latter died. The Sri Lankan date of 544 BCE for the *nirvāṇa* of Buddha is therefore preferable to the Cantonese date and will be adhered to in determining the chronology of the kings of Magadha up to Candragupta Maurya.

The Buddhist chronicles of Sri Lanka called the *Dīpavaṁsa* and the *Mahāvaṁsa* as well as the Purāṇas give detailed accounts of the royal dynasties that ruled in Magadha from the lifetime of Buddha to the time of the Mauryas. Since the Buddhists were naturally greatly interested in the events that happened in the lifetime of Buddha, the trustworthiness of their statements relating to the time of Buddha cannot be denied. As far as the account of post-Buddha kings is concerned, the Purāṇas, specially the *Vāyu* and the *Matsya,* when shorn of their mistakes, are certainly more trustworthy than the chronicles of distant Sri Lanka.

According to the Sri Lankan *Mahāvaṁsa,* King Ajātaśatru of Magadha ascended the throne eight years before the *nirvāṇa* of Buddha, i.e. in 544+8=552 BCE.[3] This one date allows us to fix the dates of all the Magadhan dynasties beginning with the one that ruled in the time of Buddha. The first king of this dynasty according to correct Purāṇic reading appears to have been Kṣemadharman (or Ksemavarman) who was successively followed by seven kings named Kṣatraujas,[4] Bimbisāra, Ajātaśatru, Darśaka, Udāyin, Nandivardhana and Mahānandin.

Unfortunately the figures of the reign periods of the first two and the last two kings of this dynaty are discrepant to a great degree even in the two most authentic Purāṇas, the *Vāyu* and the *Matsya*. The first king, Kṣemadharman, is assigned a reign period of 20[5], 36[6] or 26[7] years and his son, Kṣatraujas, 24[8] or 40[9] years. As far as the reign period of the first king is concerned, the acceptance or rejection of any of these figures does not in any way affect the chronology. We may, however, accept the figure 26 since it alone can become 36 in one recension and 20 in another. The correct figure of the reign period of the second king is clearly 24 because it is always 24 (*caturviṁśat*) which has been changed to 40 (*catvāriṁśat*) and not vice versa.[10] The last two kings, Nandivardhana and Mahānandin, are assigned a reign period of 40 years each.[11] Since Nandivardhana's father Udāyin is unanimously regarded by the Buddhists and the Jains as a son of Ajātaśatru, he must have been a brother of Darśaka, the son and successor of Ajātaśatru according to the Purāṇas. Udāyin therefore must have been a man of quite advanced age when he succeeded his brother Darśaka and a very old man when he died after a long reign of 33 years. As such, his two successors Nandivardhana and Mahānandin could hardly have ruled for the enormously long period of 40 years each. It is therefore highly probable that, as in the case of Kṣatraujas, the second king of this dynasty, the figure 40 (*catvāriṁśat*) is a mistake for 24 (*caturviṁśat*). As regards the other kings, the *Vāyu* and the *Matsya* Purāṇas differ only in the case of Ajātaśatru and Darśaka, the fourth and the fifth kings, but the difference is nominal and negligible and the lower figures may be accepted. With the removal of these discrepancies, the regnal years of the kings of this dynasty, which may be called the Haryaṅka dynasty on the authority of the ancient poet Aśvaghoṣa,[12] are as follows:

Kṣemadharman	26 years
Kṣatraujas	24 years

Bimbisāra	28 years
Ajātaśatru	25 years
Darśaka	24 years
Udāyin	33 years
Nandivardhana	24 years
Mahānandin	24 years

The most powerful contemporaries of the Haryaṅka kings of Magadha were the Pradyotas of Avantī. By placing Śiśunāga and his son Kākavarṇi after them, the Purāṇas indirectly support the Buddhist account according to which the Haryaṅka dynasty was followed by the Śiśunāga dynasty. Śiśunāga is unanimously assigned a reign period of 40 years by the Purāṇas and his son Kākavarṇi is assigned a reign period of 26 years by the *Matsya Purāṇa* which seems to have preserved the correct reading. The total reign period of the Śiśunāgas, if we accept the reading of what Pargiter calls the "b" *Vāyu* manuscript[13] was 65 years. The difference of one year between the actual aggregate of the two reigns and the total assigned to the dynasty may be accounted for by the probability that the reign period of Śiśunāga was actually 39 years and some months and was rounded off as 40 years.

The Śiśunāgas were succeeded by the Nandas who also ruled for two generations. The founder of this dynasty, Mahāpadma, ruled for 28 years according to the correct reading preserved in the *Vāyu Purāṇa,* and his eight sons ruled simultaneously for 12 years. They were vanquished and slain by Candragupta Maurya. We have already seen that according to reliable Buddhist evidence, king Ajātaśatru of the Haryaṅka dynasty ascended the throne in 552 BCE. This one date allows us to fix the dates of all the kings of the three dynasties that ruled in Magadha before the foundation of the Maurya empire by Candragupta. This chronology may be tabulated as follows:

Name of the Kings	*Length of reign (years)*	*Date* (BCE)
Kṣemadharman	26	630 – 604
Kṣatraujas	24	604 – 580
Bimbisāra	28	580 – 552
Ajātaśatru	25	552 – 527
Darśaka	24	527 – 503
Udāyin	33	503 – 470
Nandivardhana	24	470 – 446
Mahānandin	24	446 – 422
Śiśunāga	39	422 – 383
Kākavarṇi	26	383 – 357
Mahāpadma	28	357 – 329
The eight Nandas	12	329 – 317

According to this chronology, Candragupta, having vanquished and killed the Nandas, ascended the throne in 317 BCE and it is wonderfully correct and accurate. Scholars generally place the accession of Candragupta Maurya in 321 BCE, assuming that his conquest of Magadha and revolt against Greek authority in the Punjab must have occurred within a couple of years after the death of Alexander in 323 BCE. The evidence at our disposal shows that Candragupta attacked the Nandas after conquering the north-western borders of India.[14] The presence of Eudemos in the Punjab till 317 BCE, however, shows that Candragupta could not have been in possession of the north-west frontier of India before that date. Candragupta, therefore, must have conquered the Punjab and the Nanda empire in 317 BCE.

This date also agrees with the synchronism of Aśoka with the Greek kings mentioned in his Rock Edict XIII. Candragupta reigned for 24 years and thus must have been succeeded by his son Bindusāra in 293 BCE. Since Bindusāra ruled for 25 years, the date of Aśoka's accession would be 268 BCE. The chronology of the *Mahāvaṁsa* is, as already pointed out, untrustworthy and its assertion that Aśoka was formally inaugurated four years after his accession cannot be accepted as correct, as it is not supported by any other evidence. In fact the Purāṇas and all the other sources for the history of Aśoka do not mention any such interval, and Aśoka's calculation of dates from his *abhiṣeka* does not necessarily mean, as pointed out by Professor Bhandarkar,[15] that there was an interval between that event and his father's death. This date of Aśoka's accession is in complete agreement with the dates of the Greek kings mentioned in his edict. This edict was engraved 13 years after Aśoka's *abhiṣeka*, i.e. in 268-13=255 BCE. At this date all the kings were alive as can be seen from their dates given below:

Antiochus Theos of Syria	261 – 246 BCE
Ptolemy Philadelphus of Egypt	285 – 247 BCE
Antigonus Gonatus of Macedonia	276 – 239 BCE
Magas of Cyrene	*c*. 300 – 250 BCE
Alexander of Epirus	reigned up to 255 BCE

Let us now examine the chronological data of the Buddhist chronicles of Sri lanka. According to their own evidence Ajātaśatru, the son of the famous Bimbisāra, ascended the throne in 552 BCE. The reign periods of kings from Ajātaśatru to the Nandas as given in the *Mahāvaṁsa* are as follows:

Ajātaśatru	32 years
Udāyi-bhadda	16 years

Anuruddha and Muṇḍa	8 years
Nāgadāsaka	24 years
Susunāga	18 years
Kālāsoka	28 years
Kālāsoka's sons	22 years
Nandas	22 years

The total of these reigns comes to 170 years. Thus according to this chronology, Candragupta mounted the throne 170 years after the accession of Ajātaśatru, that is to say in 552-170=382 BCE. This date is patently absurd. We must, therefore, adhere to the Purāṇic chronology as elucidated above.

A word may also be said about the chronology of the kings of the Maurya dynasty who succeeded Aśoka. The Purāṇic lists of Maurya kings appear confused and contradictory at first sight. But if we patiently and critically examine them, the confusion and contradictions are removed. Aśoka's eldest son was Kuṇāla according to all our sources. The son and successor of Kuṇāla according to the *Matsya Purāṇa* was Daśaratha, who though not mentioned by the Jains and Buddhists, is known to have ruled in Magadha soon after Aśoka by his inscriptions in the Nāgārjuni hill caves. Daśaratha was according to the same *Purāṇa* succeeded by Samprati. According to the *Vāyu* and *Brahmāṇḍa* Purāṇas, on the other hand, the son and successor of Kuṇāla was Bandhupālita who in turn was succeeded by Indrapālita. It seems that the *de facto* ruler during the reign of Daśaratha was his brother Samprati and for this reason Daśaratha was called Bandhupālita, i.e. one protected by his brother. That appears to be the reason why the Buddhists and the Jains omit the name of Daśaratha and mention Samprati alone as the son and successor of Kuṇāla. Indrapālita seems to have been another name of Samprati.

Some scholars read the name of a king named Daśona in the Purāṇic lists of Maurya kings. As a matter of fact no such king is known to the Purāṇas. The *Matsya Purāṇa* list of Maurya kings contains a corrupt line which is as follows: *saptānām daśa varṣāṇi tasya naptā bhaviṣyati*. Here *saptānām* seems to be a mistake for *suyaṣāḥ* another name of Kuṇāla according to the *Viṣṇu* and *Bhāgavata* Purāṇas. This line by metathesis of the first two words has been further corrupted into *daśonaḥ sapta varṣāṇi teṣām naptā bhaviṣyati* in what Pargiter calls the e *Vāyu Purāṇa*. To see the name of a king named Daśona in this line is therefore completely unjustified.

The names Daśaratha and Samprati mentioned in the *Matsya Purāṇa* also occur in the e *Vāyu Purāṇa*. The son and successor of Samprati according to the e *Vāyu Purāṇa* was Śāliśuka, whose reality is proved by his mention in the *Yuga Purāṇa* section of *Gārgī Saṁhitā*. Śāliśuka's son Devavarman is known to the *Vāyu* and *Brahmāṇḍa* as well as the *Viṣṇu* and *Bhāgavata* Purāṇas, though the last two call him Somasarman. Devavarman's son Śatadhanvan is known to all the Purāṇas, as is the last King Bṛhadratha who is also mentioned by Bāṇa in his *Harṣacarita*.

Most of the Purāṇas say at the end of the account of the Mauryan dynasty that there were in all nine Maurya kings who ruled for a total period of 137 years. If we leave out the name of Kuṇāla who was according to all accounts blind and therefore most probably never ruled, the number of kings in the Purāṇic lists is actually nine and the aggregate of their reign periods is also 137 years as the following table shows:

Name of King	*Length of reign (years)*	*Date* (BCE)
Candragupta	24	317 – 293
Bindusāra	25	293 – 268

Aśoka	36	268 – 232
Daśaratha (Bandhupālita)	8	232 – 224
Samprati (Indrapālita)	9	224 – 215
Śāliśuka	13	215 – 202
Devavarman	7	202 – 195
Śatadhanvan	8	195 – 187
Bṛhadratha	7	187 – 180
Total	137	317 – 180

Sources

The variety and abundance of the material at our disposal for writing the history of Candragupta Maurya and his times is fortunately such as we do not get for any other period of Indian history before the establishment of the Mughal empire under Akbar. Brāhmaṇical, Buddhist, Jain and classical authors vie with each other in providing rich information about the period. This information is also supplemented by inscriptions.

Of the Brāhmaṇical works five of the Purāṇas, namely *Matsya, Vāyu, Brahmāṇḍa, Viṣṇu* and *Bhāgavata* give lists of Mauryan and pre-Mauryan kings. The most important Brāhmaṇical work which throws abundant light on Mauryan polity is the *Arthaśāstra* of Kauṭilya whose date has unfortunately been a subject of keen controversy, a brief notice of which will be taken at the end of this chapter. The other Brāhmaṇical works of a later age and doubtful historical value are the celebrated drama *Mudrārākṣasa* composed by the poet Viśākha-datta in the eighth century CE and the two collections of stories, the *Bṛhatkathāmañjarī* of Kṣemendra and the *Kathāsaritsāgara* of Somadeva. Both of them, though based on the ancient Prākṛt *Bṛhatkathā*, were composed in the eleventh century CE.

Among Buddhist works the most important are the two chronicles of Sri Lanka called the *Dīpavaṁsa* and the *Mahāvaṁsa* composed in the fourth and the sixth century CE respectively. Two later works are the *Mahābodhivaṁsa* and the *Mahāvaṁsaṭīkā*. Important light on the genesis of the Mauryas is also thrown by the ancient *Mahāparinibbāna Sutta* and the Sanskrit work *Divyāvadāna*.

Among Jain works the earliest is the *Kalpasūtra* believed to have been composed by Bhadrabāhu, a contemporary of Candragupta. Another important Jain work is the *Pariśiṣṭaparvan* of Hemacandra composed in Sanskrit in the twelfth century CE.

The Greek and Latin works on India may be divided into two categories. To the first category belong the writings of three of the companions of Alexander on his campaigns in the north-western part of India, namely Nearchus, Onesicritus, and Aristobulus. To the second category belongs the work of Megasthenes who was sent as ambassador to the court of Candragupta and utilized his time in writing an account of India and the Mauryan court under the title of *Indika*. The original writings of Megasthenes and his predecessors have been lost but extracts from them have been preserved in the writings of Greek and Roman authors who lived between the first century BCE and the second century CE. The most noted of these authors were Strabo, Diodorus, Pliny, Arrian, Appian, Plutarch, Curtius and Justin. Schwanbeck has with great ability and industry, collected all the dispersed fragments of the *Indika* of Megasthenes. McCrindle has done the useful work of translating into English all the Greek accounts of India and publishing them in separate books entitled *Invasion of India by Alexander*, *Ancient India in Classical Literature*, and *Ancient India : Megasthenes and Arrian*. Whatever in this account of early Greek writers and particularly of Megasthenes, as preserved in the works of later Greek authors, is based on the personal observation of the writer is undoubtedly most valuable, though the pieces of information based either on hearsay or on the misunderstanding or imagination of the writer are to be taken with a pinch of salt.

Age of the *Arthaśāstra*

The *Arthaśāstra* is attributed to the first Maurya emperor's famous Chancellor whose personal name was Viṣṇugupta but who was better known by his patronymic Cāṇakya and *gotra* or family name Kauṭilya.[16] A great controversy has raged around the authorship and date of the *Arthaśāstra*. Dr. Shamasastry who discovered, edited and translated the book into English for the first time gave very sound arguments to prove the genuineness of the work and H. Jacobi and V.A. Smith concurred with him. Later, however, a number of scholars like Jolly, Keith, Winternitz, O. Stein, F.W. Thomas, and E.H. Johnston pronounced the work to be a piece of forgery of about the third century CE. Their arguments were forcefully refuted by K.P. Jayaswal and Ganapati Sastri, the latter having brought out a fresh edition of the text with an excellent commentary. J.J. Meyer who translated the work into German and later Breloer and Nilakanta Sastri also very ably demonstrated that the arguments of Keith, Jolly, and others cannot stand the test of scrutiny and that there is not even a single convincing argument against the ascription of the book to the chancellor of the first Maurya emperor. On the other hand the main features of government set forth in the book wonderfully agree with the description of Megasthenes and the differences in details are due to the theoretical character of the book. Moreover, several early writers refer to Cāṇakya as a writer on statecraft, and Daṇḍin, while referring to the work of Cāṇakya mentions even its size which agrees exactly with the size mentioned in the *Arthaśāstra* itself. Some of the Sanskrit works, notably the *Yājñavalkya Smṛti*, are indebted to the *Arthaśāstra* in a considerable measure. Lastly, not only the

Girnar inscription of Rudradāman belonging to CE 150, but also the inscriptions of Aśoka mention technical terms occurring in the *Arthaśāstra*, thus proving its genuineness.

Notes

1. *Asiatic Researches*, Vol. IV, pp. 10-11.
2. The Jain author Hemacandra who lived in the twelfth century CE gives the date 467 BCE for the demise of Mahāvīra, but as this date goes against the clear statement of the Buddhist *Dīgha Nikāya* and *Majjhima Nikāya*, according to which Mahāvīra died before Buddha, it cannot be accepted.
3. *Mahāvaṁsa*, V.
4. He is called Kṣemajit by the *Matsya Purāṇa*. Some scholars like Turnour and N.L. Dey, relying on Buddhist sources, mention Bhaṭṭiya as his name. As rightly observed by Dr. Raychaudhury (*Political History of Ancient India*, p. 117) Bhaṭṭiya may have been an epithet comparable to Seniya and Kūniya of Bimbisāra and Ajātaśatru respectively.
5. *Vāyu* 99; *Brahmāṇḍa* III, 74.
6. *Matsya*, 272.
7. This figure occurs in what Pargiter calls the n *Matsya*.
8. *Matsya*, 272.
9. *Vāyu* 99; *Brahmāṇḍa* III, 74.
10. Since the word *caturviṁśat* is grammatically wrong, the correct word being *caturviṁśati*, copyists sometimes changed it to *catvāriṁśat*.
11. The best reading is found in the n *Matsya* which is as follows: *Catvāriṁśat samā bhāvyo rājā vai Nandivardhanaḥ*

    Catvāriṁśat tataś caiva Mahānandī bhaviṣyati.
12. *Buddhacarita* XI, 2.
13. According to this text the total reign period of the Śiśunāgas is said to have been : *etāni trīṇi varṣāṇi dviṣaṣṭyabhyadhikāni tu; Śiśunāgā bhaviṣyanti rājānah kṣatra bandhavaḥ*, i.e. Śiśunāgas, the kinsfolk of the Kṣatriyas, will be kings for these 65 years. The use of the word Śiśunāgas in plural was no doubt originally meant to include the brief reign of the young children of Kākavarṇi under the guardianship of Nanda.

14. The story of Candragupta and the old woman which suggests this fact is found in the Jain *Pariśiṣṭaparvan* as well as the Buddhist *Mahāvaṁsaṭīkā*. *Vide* chapter 8.

15. Bhandarkar, *Aśoka*, pp. 9-10.

16. Kauṭili (a variant of Kauṭilya) is mentioned in the *Matsya Purāṇa* as one of the *gotras* in the *Vatṣa pakṣa* of the Bhārgavas and seems to be derived from Koṭila.

2

Rise and Growth of the Kingdom of Magadha

JANAMEJAYA, the celebrated Paurava-Bhārata monarch of the kingdom of Kuru, was the first Indo-Āryan ruler who sowed the seeds of the unification of India under one sceptre, by carving out a large kingdom in the north-west of India towards the end of the eleventh century BCE. But the calamity which befell the Kuru kingdom only four generations later, led to the migration of the descendants of Janamejaya to the Vatsa region around the city of Prayāga in what is now the state of Uttar Pradesh in India.

It was only four centuries later towards the close of the seventh century BCE, when the mantle of Kuru fell on Magadha, that the seeds sown by Janamejaya showed signs of sprouting. It was a period of revolutionary changes in all spheres, religious, social and political. The birth of the Teachers of two great religions was the signal for the advent of new ideas in the religious and social spheres, while the rise of big kingdoms heralded the ensuing transformation in the political conditions of the country.

According to the Buddhist *Aṅguttara Nikāya*, there were sixteen *mahājanapadas* or large states in India at the end of the seventh and the beginning of the sixth century BCE. They were from east to west Aṅga, Magadha, Vajji, Malla, Kāśī, Kosala, Vatsa, Cedi, Kuru, Pañcāla, Śūrasena, Matsya, Avantī, Aśmaka,

Gāndhāra and Kāmboja. Most of these states were monarchies, but some were republics. Thus Vajji was a confederacy of eight republican clans. Malla, Kuru, and Pañcāla may also have been republics. The other republican clans of this period were the Śākyas, the Koliyas, the Kālāmas, the Bulis, the Bhaggas, and the Moriyas.

The most powerful states at the beginning of the sixth century BCE were the four kingdoms of Kosala, Vatsa, Magadha and Avantī. Two of these kingdoms, Kosala and Vatsa, were still being ruled by scions of their ancient dynasties. But in the other two, their ancient dynasties were uprooted and replaced by new ones.

Kosala, which corresponded to the modern Avadh region of the state of Uttar Pradesh, was being ruled by kings of the Ikṣvāku dynasty who claimed descent from Rāma, the hero of the *Rāmāyaṇa*. The capital of this kingdom was the famous city of Śrāvastī. The kingdom of Vatsa which lay to the south of Kosala around the holy city of Prayāga was being ruled by the descendants of Janamejaya whose capital was the city of Kauśāmbī.

Magadha, which corresponded to the Patna and Gayā districts of south Bihar, was brought under Āryan rule ten generations before the great Bhārata war by a prince of the Paurava-Bhārata family named Bṛhadratha. It was probably Kṣemadharman, the grandfather of the celebrated king, Bimbisāra, who vanquished Ripuñjaya, the last ruler of the dynasty of Bṛhadratha around the time of the birth of Buddha and established a new dynasty which according to the poet Aśvaghoṣa bore the name Haryaṅka. The capital of Magadha was Girivraja.

Kṣemadharman was succeeded by his son who is called Kṣatraujas or Kṣemajit by the Purāṇas and Bhaṭṭiya by Buddhist writers. It is at this stage that the history of Northern India emerges from semi-darkness to daylight. The Sri Lankan *Mahāvaṁsa* informs us that Bimbisāra was anointed king by his own father when he was only fifteen years old. Looking to the young age of Bimbisāra, it appears that immediately after his accession to the throne, Kṣatraujas delegated all power to his son who was thus the *de facto* ruler of Magadha during the 24 years of his father's reign and the 28 years of his own reign. Bimbisāra thus ruled over Magadha for 52 years as mentioned in the *Mahāvaṁsa*. Bimbisāra laid the foundation of Magadhan imperialism. He married Kosalā Devī, the daughter of King Mahākosala and sister of King Prasenajīt of Kosala, and she brought as dowry a part of Kāśī which at that time was included in the Kosala kingdom. Thus the limits of the kingdom of Magadha were extended in the west as far as Kāśī. In the east Bimbisāra defeated Brahmadatta, king of Aṅga, and annexed his kingdom. According to Jain sources, Bimbisāra's son Kūṇika or Ajātaśatru was appointed viceroy of the new territory with his headquarters at the city of Campā. Bimbisāra built a palace near the old capital Girivraja and a new city grew around it which came to be called Rājagṛha.

The most powerful rival of Magadha was Avantī. According to the Purāṇas, after the passing away of the Bṛhadrathas of Magadha, a minister named Pulaka, having killed his master, anointed his son Pradyota as king over the lands of the Vītihotras (eastern Mālwā) and the Avantīs (western Mālwā). As the dynasty of Pradyota ruled for 138 years and was uprooted by King Śiśunāga of Magadha as soon as he ascended the throne in 422 BCE, Pradyota must have begun his rule in 422 + 138 = 560 BCE when Bimbisāra was still on the throne of Magadha. According to the Purāṇas he brought the rulers of neighbouring states under his subjection. His epithet Mahāsena indicates that he had a large army at his disposal.

Bimbisāra was succeeded by his son Ajātaśatru in 552 BCE. The latter was an ambitious monarch and, according to Buddhist accounts, removed his father from the throne. He waged many wars with Prasenajīt, the aged king of Kosala, when the latter confiscated the district of Kāśī after the death of Bimbisāra and Kosalā Devī. At last Prasenajīt was constrained to conclude a treaty according to which he married his daughter to Ajātaśatru ceding the district of Kāśī which became an integral part of Magadha. Ajātaśatru attacked and defeated the Vajjis also and annexed their territory, which included the cities of Vaiśālī and Mithilā, to his dominions.

Both Mahāvīra and Gautama Buddha, the real founders of Jainism and Buddhism respectively,[1] died in the reign of Ajātāśatru after making revolutionary changes in the religious and social ideas and practices of the people of India. Ajātaśatru became a devotee of Buddha and is said to have expressed repentance to the great Teacher for his misbehaviour against his own father Bimbisāra. Only a few weeks after the demise of Buddha, the first Buddhist council met under the presidentship of Mahākaśyapa and the patronage of Ajātaśatru.

Ajātaśatru was succeeded by his son Darśaka in 527 BCE. The important position which the kingdom of Magadha occupied during the reign of King Darśaka is revealed by the celebrated Sanskrit drama *Svapnavāsavadattam* composed by the ancient poet Bhāsa. According to this play, King Udayana of Vatsa was under threat of attack by an enemy. His wise miṁster Yaugandharāyaṇa felt that the threat could be averted only with the help of the mighty king of Magadha and the best way of getting that help was a matrimonial alliance between the two royal families. Padmāvatī, the sister of king Darśaka, was noted for her beauty. Yaugandharāyaṇa wanted King Udayana to marry her. Udayana, however, was deeply attached to his queen, Vāsavadattā, the charming daughter of King Pradyota. Yaugandharāyaṇa took the noble queen, Vāsavadattā, into confidence and went to a village where he spread the rumour that both of them were consumed in a conflagration. Udayana, thinking that Vāsavadattā was dead, condescended to marry Padmāvatī. Yaugandharāyaṇa and Vāsavadattā then came out of their hiding and Udayana was successful in defeating his enemy with the help of King Darśaka.

Darśaka was succeeded by Udāyin in 503 BCE. The Buddhist and Jain works make him a son of Ajātaśatru; which means that he was a brother of Darśaka who probably died without a son. Udāyin was a famous king and according to Purāṇic accounts, which are supported by Jain evidence,[2] he built a city named Kusumapura or Pāṭaliputra on the southern bank of the Gaṅgā in the fourth year of his reign, i.e. in about 500 BCE and made it his capital. This city was destined not only to become the capital of one of the greatest empires of history, but also to withstand the test of time for about 2500 years, for under the name of Patna it still retains a semblance of its ancient glory as the capital of the large state of Bihar.

Udāyin died in 470 BCE and was succeeded by his son who is called Nandivardhana by the Purāṇas and Anuruddha by the Sri Lankan *Mahāvaṁsa*. No event of his reign is, however, known to us.

Nandivardhana-Anuruddha was succeeded in 446 BCE by his son who is called Mahānandin in the Purāṇas and Muṇḍa in Buddhist works. The *Aṅguttara Nikāya* mentions a tragic incident of his life which brought him under Buddhist influence. When his wife Bhadrā died, he was beside with grief but the teachings of a Buddhist monk brought solace to him.

Mahānandin, the Muṇḍa of Buddhist accounts, was the last king of his dynasty according to the Purāṇas. The *Mahāvaṁsa* of Sri Lanka, however, mentions a king named Nāgadāsaka as his son and successor. This king is not known to any Indian work, Hindu, Buddhist, or Jain. The mention of Nāgadāsaka as a son and successor of Muṇḍa by the *Mahāvaṁsa* is therefore certainly an error. It is possible that the full name of the founder of the next dynasty was Śiśunāgadāsa, and Nāgadāsaka was only a variant of this name, for both the words have the same meaning, "little slave of the Nāgas." If so, the Sri Lankan chroniclers must have mistakenly turned these names into two separate kings.[3] Whatever be the case, there is no doubt that both the Sri Lankan chronicles and the Purāṇas place Śiśunāga at the same period of time, for according to the former he destroyed the fourth successor of King Ajātaśatru, and according to the latter he destroyed the fourth successor of Ajātaśatru's contemporary Pradyota.

It appears that the last king of the Haryaṅka dynasty was a weakling and was, after 24 years of reign, slain by Śiśunāga who then mounted the throne in 422 BCE. The latter was a powerful ruler. He placed his son in Vārāṇasī, probably as governor of the province of Kāśī, and restored the city of Girivraja to its former glory as the capital of Magadha. Whether he moved to Girivraja for strategic reasons or because of Pāṭaliputra's association with the old dynasty, we do not know. Soon after ascending the throne, he set out for conquest. According to the Purāṇas he destroyed the glory of the Pradyotas, which no doubt means that he defeated them and annexed the region of Avantī to the growing Magadha kingdom. If Śiśunāga conquered and annexed Avantī, he could hardly have spared the intervening kingdoms of Kosala and Vatsa. This is fully supported by Purāṇic genealogies according to which the dynasties that ruled over Magadha, Avantī, Kosala, and Vatsa about the time of the *nirvāṇa* of Buddha ended practically after the same number of generations. The Magadhan dominions in the time of Śiśunāga thus became large enough to be called an empire and Śiśunāga became the first Indian king who could legitimately be called an emperor.

Śiśunāga was succeeded in 383 BC by his son who is called Kākavarṇi by the Purāṇas and Kālāśoka by the Sri Lankan chroniclers. It appears that his real name was Aśoka, but because of his dark complexion he was nicknamed Kālāśoka or the black Aśoka and Kākavarṇi or the crow-coloured. He restored Pāṭaliputra to its former position as the capital of Magadha. He was a patron of Buddhism and the second Buddhist council met during his reign under the presidentship of Yaśa.

Though the two kings of the new dynasty were able and powerful rulers, there was a hostile group of people in their kingdom who in course of time succeeded in overthrowing the dynasty. The leader of this group was a person who bore the name Nanda. According to the *Harṣacarita* of Bāṇa, Kākavarṇi Śaiśunāgi had a dagger thrust into his throat in the vicinity of his capital city. This must have been the act of that group whose leader was Nanda. According to the Purāṇas, he was a son of Mahānandin by a śūdra woman. He must have, therefore, considered Śiśunāga and Kākavarṇi as usurpers and must have been looking for an opportunity to seize the throne of which he considered himself the rightful owner.

The origin of King Nanda has been a subject of keen controversy among scholars. As we have already seen, the Purāṇas unanimously regard him as a son of Udāyiṇ's grandson Mahānandin by a śūdra woman. The late Jain work *Pariśiṣṭaparvan* on the other hand represents Nanda as the son of a courtesan by a barber. Classical writers have given a similar pedigree to Alexander's Magadhan contemporary. Thus Curtius has given a fairy tale-like account explaining how Nanda though the son of a barber became a powerful ruler. The question naturally arises as to which of these accounts of the origin of Nanda is true and how the wrong versions originated. Let us examine this question in some detail.

We have already seen that the Purāṇas unanimously regard Nanda as the illegitimate son of the last descendant of Bimbisāra. This provides a convincing reason for the destruction of the Śiśunāgas by Nanda who must have considered them as usurpers. The Jain and classical accounts of the origin of Nanda, though similar, differ in their details which naturally makes their authenticity doubtful. The question, however, still remains that if Nanda was the son of Mahānandin, the last descendant of Bimbisāra, how he has been represented as the son of a barber by the classical and Jain writers.

We have already said that King Mahānandin of the Purāṇas must be identified with King Muṇḍa of the Buddhist accounts. It is quite likely that this king had two names but, of the two, the name Muṇḍa was better known and more popular. One of the meanings of the word Muṇḍa in Sanskrit is barber. It is quite within the range of probability that in distant Punjab some people thought that Nanda's father Muṇḍa was really a barber, and on the basis of the information given to them the Greek writers have called the king of Pāṭaliputra as the son of a barber. When once a story, however wrong, gains currency it is repeated by later writers and that is how the Jain *Pariśiṣṭaparvan* also calls Nanda the son of a barber. That such a mistake was quite possible can be proved from another instance. According to Bhāsa's *Svapna-vāsavadattam*, Pradyota had two sons named Gopāla and Pālaka, and Āryaka, one of the kings of the Pradyota dynasty according to the Purāṇas, was apparently a son of Pradyota's son Gopāla. The famous play, *Mṛcchakaṭikam*, has, however, turned Āryaka into a cowherd boy because the author of this work misunderstood the name Gopāla as meaning a cowherd. The name Muṇḍa could similarly have been misunderstood as meaning a barber. It should further be remembered that neither the Purāṇas and other Hindu works mentioning Nanda, nor the Buddhist works of India and Sri Lanka, nor even the ancient Jain works describe Nanda as the son of a barber. The barber ancestry of Nanda is thus proved to be a mistake arising out of a misunderstanding and no doubt whatever remains is that he was really a son of Mahānandin-Muṇḍa and ascended the throne of Magadha after assassinating Kākavarṇi, the son of the usurper Śiśunāga.

Nanda was probably a posthumous son of Mahānandin, and must have been 65 years of age when he assassinated Kākavarṇi-Kālāśoka in 357 BC. According to the account given by Curtius, after killing his predecessor, he usurped the supreme authority under the pretence of acting as guardian to the royal children and then put the young princes to death. The *Mahāvaṁsa* gives the number of these princes as 10, but mistakenly assigns them a reign of 22 years. The fact that they were still 'young' when they were put to death clearly means that the period during which Nanda ruled in their name could not have been of more than a few months.

According to the Purāṇas, King Nanda was popularly known by the name Mahāpadma or Mahāpadmapati, meaning lord of immense wealth. The *Mahābodhivaṁsa* on the other hand calls him Ugrasena meaning one having a formidable army. These epithets clearly prove that Nanda was a very powerful king. According to the Purāṇas he exterminated all the Kṣatriya dynasties that still retained their independence and became the sole monarch of the territories conquered by him. The Kṣatriya dynasties whose territories were incorporated in the growing Magadhan empire from time to time were, according to the Purāṇas, the Ikṣvākus (of Kosala), the Pañcālas, the Kaśeyas (of Kāśī), the Haihayas (of Avantī), the Kaliṅgas, the Aśmakas, the Kurus, the Maithilas (of Mithilā), the Sūrasenas, and the Vītihotras (of eastern Mālwā). To these may be added the Paurava-Bhāratas of Vatsa whose name seems to have been inadvertently omitted. Of the territories of these Kṣatriya families, Kāśī, Mithilā, Avantī, eastern Mālwā, and probably Kosala and Vatsa already formed part of the Magadhan empire when Mahāpadma Nanda seized the throne. The other five, namely Kuru, Pañcāla, Śūrasena, Kaliṅga, and Aśmaka were definitely conquered by Māhāpadma Nanda. The inclusion of Kuru, Pañcāla, and Śūrasena in the Nanda dominions is proved by the testimony of classical writers according to whom all the regions of India to the east of the river Beās were under one king. According to Curtius, the region beyond Beās was inhabited by two nations, the Gangaridae and the Prassii. The Gangaridae seem to have been inhabitants of the Ganges delta, i.e. Bengal. The word Prassii is clearly a corruption of the Sanskrit Prācya meaning people of the eastern region which primarily meant Magadha and its neighbourhood but was probably at this period applicable to most of the region east of the Beās. The conquest of Kaliṅga which roughly corresponds to modern Orissa by Mahāpadma Nanda is proved by the Hāthigumphā inscription of King Khāravela according to which King Nanda constructed some irrigation works in Kaliṅga and brought the idol of a Jain Tīrthaṅkara from there. The conquest of Aśmaka in the Godāvarī valley by Mahāpadma is made probably by the existence on the Godāvarī of a city called Nau Nand Dehra. Thus the conquests of Mahāpadma made him the sole monarch of the vast regions stretching from the Himālayas to the Godāvarī.

Mahāpadma Nanda had a long reign of 28 years and died in 329 BCE at the ripe old age of 93 years. He was not only a great conqueror but also a capable ruler. The country prospered during his reign. A galaxy of scholars among whom the most noted was the grammarian Kātyāyana are believed to have flourished during his reign.

Mahāpadma had eight sons, the eldest of whom is called by the Purāṇas Sukalpa, Sumālya, or Sahalya. As pointed out by

Dr. Barua, the correct name is Sahalya which is closest to the Sahālin of the *Divyāvadāna*. The Greeks who accompanied Alexander do not know the name Sahalya, but call the king of eastern India as Agrammes which is, as Dr. Raychaudhury rightly says, a distorted form of Augrasainya, i.e. son of Ugrasena, the first Nanda. It appears that though Sahalya was the *de jure* king, his brothers shared sovereign power with him, because the Purāṇas seem to indicate that all the eight Nandas ruled simultaneously. This finds support in the accounts of Greek writers. Thus although Curtius and Diodorus mention the name of the king of Prassii as Agrammes and Xandrammes, Plutarch speaks of the kings of Prassii in plural.[4]

Sahalya and his brothers were according to all our sources very powerful and rich. According to classical writers they had an army of two hundred thousand infantry, at least twenty thousand cavalry, three thousand elephants and two thousand four-horsed chariots.[5] The possession of huge wealth by them is attested by many sources. According to a passage of the *Kathāsaritsāgara,* they possessed 990 million gold pieces.[6] The Chinese pilgrim Hieun Tsang, who visited India in the seventh century CE, refers to "the five treasures of King Nanda's seven precious substances."[7] They were, however, very unpopular. They were hated because of their lack of ability to rule over their vast dominions, their heterodox disposition, and their greedy nature. The possession of such a huge amount of wealth by them probably implies a great deal of extortion on the part of the Nandas. The lowness of the birth of Mahāpadma perhaps did not bother the people because of his great ability, but the misrule of the later Nandas brought their low origin into prominence in the eyes of the people.

There are reasons to believe that the great empire built by Mahāpadma Nanda showed signs of disintegration during the period of his sons' rule. The kingdom of Kaliṅga certainly regained its independence, for if it had remained a part of the Nanda empire, it is unlikely that it could have escaped the iron grip of Candragupta, whose absence of control over it is implied in a passage in one of the inscriptions of his grandson Aśoka, its conqueror.[8] With their immense wealth and large army the Nandas were, however, still powerful enough to retain most of their empire intact.

To get a full picture of India in the time of the Nandas, we must also cast a glance over the regions outside the Nanda empire. These regions were, on the one hand, the part of India south of the river Godāvarī and, on the other hand, the part of the country north-west of the river Sarasvatī which flowed through what is now Haryana before it disappeared in the desert of Rajasthan. Unfortunately, we know little about the political condition of the region south of the Godāvarī in the time of the Nandas. We are, however, lucky in possessing a good account of the north-western region of India written by the companions of the Macedonian invader Alexander and preserved for us by the later Greek and Roman writers.

In the latter half of the fourth century BCE, a king named Philip ruled over a small country named Macedonia which lay to the north of Greece. He, however, conquered Greece and thus enlarged his kingdom. His ambitious son Alexander, on acceding to the throne, set out with his army for the conquest of the world. Having subjugated the Persian empire, he crossed the Hindu Kush Mountains in 327 BCE. In the valley of the rivers Kunar and Swāt, he for the first time encountered an Indian tribe named Assakenoi or Āśvakāyanas, the ancestors of the modern Afghans. The Āśvakāyanas gave the invader a tough resistance and bravely defended their city of Massaga or Maśakāvatī but were ultimately defeated.

Alexander appointed Nicanor as satrap of the hilly region west of the Indus. He then proceeded to Puṣkalāvatī, the capital of western Gāndhāra, which had already been conquered by a part of his army he had sent towards this city when he was fighting with the Āśvakāyanas. Alexander left a part of his army in Puṣkalāvatī under an officer named Philip. Between Puṣkalāvatī and the river Indus, Alexander conquered many small towns, the most famous of which was Aornos which seems to be identical with the Varaṇā of Pāṇini.[9] Here also Alexander left a part of his army under the leadership of an Indian named Śaśigupta.

In the spring of 326 BCE, Alexander crossed the river Sindhu or Indus and entered into India proper. The condition of the Indus valley consisting of the two provinces of the Punjab and Sindh was unfortunately by no means uncongenial to the invader. It was divided into a number of small states whose mutual jealousies prevented them from uniting against the invader. As the gateway of India stood the famous city of Takṣaśilā or Taxila near the modern Rāwalpiṇḍī. It was a centre of both commerce and learning. It was at that time ruled by a king named Āmbhi, who gave a good reception to the invader regarding it as a golden opportunity for revenge against his neighbour and rival Porus. The kingdom of Āmbhi extended from the river Sindhu or Indus to the river Vitastā or Jhelum, the Hydaspes of the Greeks. On the other side of the Jhelum lay the kingdom of Kekaya which was under the rule of a king whom the Greeks have mentioned by the name of Porus which is no doubt a corrupt form of the dynastic name Paurava. To Alexander's message asking him to meet the invader, he had sent a defiant reply saying that he would meet him at the frontiers of his territory, but in arms.

Alexander then advanced against the Paurava. There was a battle on the banks of the Jhelum, but though the Paurava and his men fought bravely, Alexander succeeded in vanquishing them. The reasons for the defeat of the Paurava were plain. In the first place, he should have taken the offensive instead of waiting for the attack of the enemy. Secondly, nature herself turned against him, for, on account of heavy rains, the battlefield became muddy in which chariots began to sink and the bows of the infantry began to slip. Thirdly, the cavalry of the Paurava was inadequate compared to that of Alexander, for on a rainy day like that the mobile cavalry was much more useful than infantry, chariots or elephants. Fourthly, the Paurava had put his entire army in the field whereas Alexander had left some divisions on the other side of the Jhelum, who crossed over and gave a fresh strength to his army.

The Paurava mounted on an elephant continued to fight for some time, but at last, condescended to meet his adversary. The two strong men coming from the ends of the earth then stood face to face.[10] Alexander was struck by the handsome appearence and majestic stature of his opponent and asked him how he would like to be treated. "Like a king," was the proud reply of the Paurava. Alexander thereupon not only reinstated him in his kingdom but added to it territory still greater in extent.

When Alexander took the field again, he invaded the Glauganikae or Glaucukāyanas, a republican clan living on the west of the river Chenāb or Asiknī, the Akesines of the Greeks. They had thirty-seven towns with a population ranging between 5,000 and 10,000. They surrendered to him and their territory was added to the kingdom of the Paurava.

Soon after his victory over the Glaucukāyanas, a message reached Alexander that the Āśvakāyanas had risen in rebellion against their governor Nicanor and slain him. Alexander sent the officer Philip to the west of the Indus and he quelled the rebellion. The ruler of Abhisāra, whose principality lay in the modern Punch and Hazara districts of the state of Jammu and Kashmir, also in the meantime surrendered to Alexander. The

Macedonian conqueror then crossed the Chenāb and obtained the surrender of another Paurava whose principality was merged in the kingdom of the great Paurava.

Alexander crossed the river Irāvatī or Rāvī, called Hydraotes by the Greeks around the August of 326 BCE and conquered the Adrastai or the Adhr̥ṣṭas dwelling in the city of Pimprama. He then entered the territory of the Kathaioi or Kaṭhas who were noted for their courage and strength as well as handsomeness. Their capital was Sangala, probably identical with the Saṅkalā of Pāṇini. They offered a very tough and determined resistance to the invader. Thousands of Kaṭhas were killed. But there were heavy losses in Alexander's army also, which so enraged the Macedonian king that he razed the city of Sangala to the ground. In the neighbourhood of the Kaṭha territory lay the kingdom of a king named Sophytes or Saubhūti who extended his hand of friendship to Alexander and gave him a right royal reception.

Crossing the land of the five rivers, Alexander arrived on the bank of the river Vipāś or Beās, the Hyphasis of Greek accounts. Here he was informed about the extent and power of the Nanda empire. This information whetted Alexander's eagerness to advance further, but his troops mutinied and refused to march further. When all his efforts to persuade them failed, Alexander proclaimed his decision to return.

Alexander returned by the same route by which he came to the Beās and reached the bank of the river Jhelum in September 326 BCE. He appointed Paurava as the ruler of the country between the Jhelum and the Beās, and gave Āmbhi the charge of the territory between the Indus and the Jhelum. He appointed Philip as the satrap of the region west of the Indus.

With a body of picked troops Alexander marched further and arrived at the confluence of the rivers Jhelum and Chenāb. Here a rustic people called the Siboi submitted to him, but another warlike people called the Agalassoi offered a stout resistance to the invader. They inflicted heavy losses on the enemy, but realizing the superior strength of the invader set fire to their own homes and perished in the flames.

When Alexander advanced further along the bank of the Chenāb, he heard about the powerful Kṣatriya clans of the Mālavas and the Kṣudrakas who lived on both sides of the lower course of the Rāvī and who were planning to join hands against the invader. Having decided to foil their plan, Alexander marched against the Mālavas with such lightning rapidity that they could neither get the help of the Kṣudrakas, nor get prepared themselves for fighting but were caught working in the fields unarmed. Many Mālavas were killed while others took shelter in the cities. These cities were also then attacked and conquered by Alexander. The Mālavas escaped from these cities also, and their last stronghold was a strongly fortified town. Here there was a fierce contest between the armies of the Mālavas and the Greeks and Alexander himself was deeply wounded. This so maddened the Greek soldiers that, when they eventually managed to conquer the fort, they did not spare any one; man, woman, or child. The Mālavas who were left alive then surrendered. The Kṣudrakas also, feeling helpless, sent their representative to Alexander with full authority to conclude a treaty with the Macedonian king. Alexander added the territories of the Mālavas and Kṣudrakas to the regions over which Philip was his satrap.

Alexander then proceeded further along the bank of the Chenāb and having vanquished some other Kṣatriya clans like the Ambaṣthas and the Vasātis arrived at the confluence of the Chenāb and the Indus. Here he founded a city which marked the southern limit of the region put in charge of Philip.

Alexander then entered into the region of Sindh. Unlike the Punjab, Sindh had no republican clans at that time, but was divided into a number of kingdoms. The first king with whom Alexander came into contact was Musicanus (Mucakunda?). At first inclined to fight, he submitted to Alexander on seeing his superior strength. The proud and patriotic Brāhmaṇas of the kingdom did not like the humiliating treaty concluded by their king with the invader. On the departure of Alexander, the king on the instigation of the Brāhmaṇas repudiated the treaty. When this news reached Alexander, he sent an officer Peithon to crush the rebellion. Peithon captured the king, who, along with his Brāhmaṇa advisers, was executed by the order of Alexander. Two more kings named Oxycanus and Sambos surrendered to Alexander. At last in July 325 BCE, Alexander arrived at a city named Pattala which was situated at a place where the Indus divided into two branches before falling into the Arabian Sea. This place was like Sparta under the rule of two kings, but when Alexander reached there he found it deserted. Alexander persuaded the people to return and built there a harbour and dockyards. He appointed Peithon as the satrap of Sindh. Alexander departed from India in September 325 BCE and passing through the desert of Makran reached Babylon where he died in 323 BCE.

Such was the condition of India when a youthful person of indomitable courage and unshakable determination named Candragupta came on the scene. There were many factors which contributed to the marvellous success of Candragupta in the difficult task of uniting the major part of India under the rule of his dynasty. In the first place the conquests of Mahāpadma Nanda and his predecessors in eastern and central India, and those of Alexander in the Punjab and Sindh destroyed the small states and the petty principalities of northern India and made the task of Candragupta easier. Secondly, the discontent of the people in the Nanda empire caused by the misrule of Sahalya and his brothers, and the not very concealed hatred of foreign rule of the freedom-loving republican clans and princes of the Punjab and Sindh, most of whom had given a stout resistance to the foreign invader, made the need of a deliverer urgent. These two factors were certainly very helpful in the rise of Candragupta. He was also lucky in getting a shrewd advisor like Cāṇakya. But above all other things, the main cause of the rise of the glorious Mauryan empire was the genius of Candragupta without which he would not have been able to take advantage of the above-mentioned factors.

Notes

1. The Jains and the Buddhists regard them as the last of their Jinas and Buddhas respectively.
2. *Pariśiṣṭaparvan*, VI, 180.
3. Another reason also for adding the name of Nāgadāsaka can be surmised. It seems that the Sri Lankan chroniclers were conversant with the tradition that the total number of kings who followed Bimbisāra in his dynasty was five. Since the name of Darśaka was missing from their lists, they made the loss good by adding the name of Nāgadāsaka.
4. McCrindle, *Invasion of India by Alexander*, p. 310.
5. Diodorus increases the number of elephants to four thousand and Plutarch to six thousand. Plutarch increases the number of cavalry and chariots also to eighty thousand and eight thousand respectively.
6. *Kathāsaritsāgara* I, IV.
7. Watters, *On Yuan Chwang's Travels in India*, II, 296.
8. In Rock Edict XIII Aśoka speaks of Kaliṅga as a country previously unconquered, which seems to mean unconquered by Aśoka's ancestors.
9. *Aṣṭādhyāyī*, IV, 2, 82.
10. The last lines of the oft-criticized poem of Rudyard Kipling provide the best commentary on this scene :

    "But there is neither East nor West,
    Border nor breed nor birth,
    When two strong men stand face to face,
    Though they come from the ends of the earth."

3

Career of Candragupta

We have seen that India was far from being a united country at the time of the invasion of Alexander the Great. But the man who in a large measure achieved this unity and did much more than that was already born. This heroic figure was Candragupta.

This great leader of men has been immortalized by a grateful posterity in lauds, tales, plays, and various other types of works in Sanskrit, Pāli, Prākr̥t, and even Greek and Latin languages. Unfortunately, however, no contemporary work including the famous *Indika* of Megasthenes survives to give us an authentic account of the "founder of the greatest Indo-Āryan dynasty known in history"[1] and even Aśoka fails to mention the very name of his grandfather in his inscriptions. Yet scraps of information obtainable from inscriptions, classical sources, and Sanskrit, Pāli, and Prākr̥t works, which are either quite ancient in date or faithfully transmit ancient material, when pieced together yield a fairly trustworthy account of the ancestry and early life of the great Maurya emperor.

According to all ancient works, Buddhist, Jain, and Hindu, the Maurya family to which Candragupta belonged was of kṣatriya extraction. The various Buddhist works which mention the name of the family to which Candragupta belonged unanimously declare it to be of kṣatriya origin. The *Mahāparinibbāna Sutta*, a portion of the Pāli canon and an early authentic work, represents the Moriyas or Mauryas as kṣatriyas and rulers of the little republic of Pipphalivana who claimed a portion of the relics of Buddha after the latter's death.[2] The Buddhist *Divyāvadāna* calls Bindusāra and Aśoka, the son and grandson respectively of Candragupta, as kṣatriyas.[3] The Buddhist *Mahāvaṁsa* calls Candragupta himself a member of the kṣatriya clan of Moriyas[4] who are represented by the *Mahāvaṁsaṭīkā* as a Himālayan offshoot of the Śākyas.[5] The *Kalpasūtra* of the Jains mentions a Mauryaputra of the Kāśyapa *gotra* which shows that the Mauryas were regarded as high class folk.[6] The Purāṇas unanimously describe them as a new dynasty unconnected with the Nandas, thus implying that they were kṣatriyas, the caste to which the king normally belonged. They, no doubt, say that śūdra kingship began with the Nandas, but it simply means that the kings of śūdra caste were not unknown from that time onwards and not that all the subsequent kings were śūdras, for the Purāṇas themselves designate the Kāṇva kings who belonged to one of the subsequent dynasties as brāhmaṇas.[7] Kauṭilya himself indirectly suggests the noble origin of his sovereign's family when he lays down that a high-born king, though weak, is better than a low-born one, though strong.[8] This tradition was also recorded in medieval inscriptions which call the Maurya family as a branch of the solar race[9] and Candragupta an abode of the usages of eminent kṣatriyas.[10] Even in modern times we are aware of a Rājpūt clan of Moris whom Tod[11] considered to be the descendants of the Mauryas.[12] In the face of this varied and overwhelming evidence, the statements of the authors of a few medieval works like the Sanskrit versions of the *Bṛhatkathā* and the play *Mudrārākṣasa* who regard Candragupta as a scion of the Nanda family, and the invention of the name Murā as the mother or grandmother of Candragupta by the late commentators of the *Viṣṇu Purāṇa* and the *Mudrārākṣasa* are totally valueless, being based on wrong information and the wild imagination of these authors and commentators.[13] There is thus no room for doubt that Candragupta belonged to the kṣatriya clan of the Moriyas.

In the sixth century BCE the Moriyas were the ruling clan of the republic of Pipphilivana. According to the *Mahāvaṁsaṭīkā* which seems to be based on truth and is supported by Jain writings at a later stage, the Moriyas were a branch of the Śākyas and were so-called because when driven by the attack of the Kosalan prince Virūdhaka, they left their original home and settled in a place which abounded in *mora*s (*mayūra*s) or peacocks.[14] When King Mahāpadma Nanda went on a campaign of conquests to extend his empire, the Moriyas must have shared the fate of other clans and monarchies. In fact, we are told by the *Mahāvaṁsaṭīkā* that Candragupta's father, whose name is unfortunately not mentioned, was the chief of the Moriya clan and was killed by a powerful *rājā*, presumably Nanda. Thereafter Candragupta's mother, who was then pregnant, ran away with her father's relatives and lived at Pāṭaliputra in disguise.

At this stage the story is wonderfully corroborated by the Jain *Pariśiṣṭaparvan* and the *Uttarādhyayana sūtra* which speak of certain peacock-tamers, living near Pāṭaliputra, whose chief's daughter bore Candragupta.[15] As the *Mahāvaṁsaṭīkā* expressly says that the Moriya queen and her relatives lived in disguise, it is easy to see that the best way to disguise themselves was to act as tamers of peacocks, which were the most familar objects for the Moriyas. Moreover, as no mention is made of Candragupta's father in the Jain version, it means that it presupposes certain events, which, as we have seen, are briefly set forth in the *Mahāvaṁsaṭīkā*. Thus it is clear from both the Buddhist and Jain accounts that the Moriya family had lost all its previous rank at the time when Candragupta was born, and Justin, the Roman author, rightly observes that Candragupta was born in humble life.[16] The date of his birth must have been around 344 BCE as at the time of Alexander's Indian campaigns in 326 BCE he was only a boy, probably not more than 18 years of age.[17]

Most of the traditions agree that Candragupta spent his boyhood in the region of Magadha. According to one version of his story, he also lived for some at the court of the later Nandas and being ill-treated plotted against them and was obliged to flee. There are several stories relating to the uncommon intelligence of Candragupta even in his boyhood. One of them may be related here with advantage:

> The king of Siṁhala sent to the court of the Nandas a cage containing a lion of wax so well made that it seemed to be real. He added a message to the effect that anyone who could make that fierce animal run without opening the cage should be acknowledged to be an exceptionally talented man. The dullness of the Nandas prevented their understanding the double meaning contained in the message, but Chandragupta, in whom some little breath yet remained, offered to undertake the task. This being allowed, he made an iron rod red hot and thrust it into the figure, as a result of which the wax soon ran and the lion disappeared.[18]

In the absence of confirmation from any other source, the veracity of the tradition associating Candragupta with the court of the Nandas is doubtful. The Buddhist and Jain legends, however independent as they are of each other, agree in informing us that Candragupta raised the banner of revolt against the misrule of the Nandas with the help of a body of intrepid persons, chief among whom were a chieftain named Parvataka[19] and a shrewd brāhmaṇa named Cāṇakya, who had on a certain occasion been insulted by one of the Nandas and who thus harboured a feeling of revenge against them. The revolt was, however, suppressed and Candragupta had to flee with his friends and helpers.

Candragupta then wandered in the northern provinces. According to Plutarch he paid a visit to Alexander also, though there is nothing to indicate that his purpose was to persuade the invader to attack the kingdom of Magadha as is held by some scholars. On the contrary, if the king whom, according to Justin, Candragupta offended was Alexander,[20] it clearly means that he castigated Alexander for robbing so many nations of their freedom, for that kind of speech alone could have led Alexander to order his execution.

Be that as it may, there can be no doubt that after leaving Magadha Candragupta did not allow the grass to grow under his feet and was busy in drawing his plans for fulfilling his mission of emancipating India. According to Justin, in the course of a few years after the death of Alexander, he collected a body of armed men and instigated the Indians to overthrow the existing government. Whether by "existing government" Justin means the Greek government of the Punjab and Sindh or the Nanda government of the Prassii (Prācī or Magadha) is immaterial, because instigating the people to overthrow the government does not mean the actual overthrow of the government. It is, however, clear both from the writings of the Buddhists and Jains and the account of Justin that Candragupta attacked the prefects of Alexander and freed the Punjab and Sindh from foreign rule before attacking and conquering the mighty Magadhan empire. A curious story found both in the *Mahāvaṁsaṭīkā* and the *Pariśiṣṭaparvan* relates that while wandering, Candragupta heard an old woman saying that the cause of his failure was that he revolted against Magadha before conquering the outer provinces and that, realizing his mistake, he made up his mind to conquer the northern provinces.[21] Justin, too, clearly implies that Candragupta had not yet conquered the Magadhan empire when he attacked the prefects of Alexander, for, had he already conquered the Magadhan empire, he would have possessed a vast array of elephants and would not have mounted a wild elephant as mentioned by Justin.[22]

It is clear from Justin's account that Candragupta achieved the freedom of the people of the Punjab and Sindh after the death of Alexander. That does not, however, necessarily mean that this freedom was achieved immediately after Alexander's death. For determining the time that elapsed between the two events, we have to cast a glance over the state of affairs immediately after the death of the Macedonian conqueror. We have already seen in the previous chapter what administrative arrangements Alexander had made in the Punjab and Sindh at the time of his departure from India. In 324 BCE Philip was murdered by his mercenary troops and Eudemos was temporarily appointed in his place, but the death of Alexander in 323 BCE removed all chances of the arrangements being renewed. At the time of the second partition of the empire in 321 BCE the arrangement was continued unaltered, although Peithon, the satrap of Sindh, was transferred to the provinces situated to the west of the river Indus. The Indians were, however, growing intolerant of the domineering foreigners and the treacherous murder of Porus by Eudemos in 317 BCE was the signal for revolt. Candragupta headed the revolt and Eudemos, finding the country too hot for him, quitted India. The Greek officers and soldiers who still remained in India were put to the sword and Candragupta became the unquestioned master of the Punjab and Sindh.

With his resources and the strength of his army augmented by the conquest of the Punjab and Sindh, Candragupta wasted no time in mobilizing his army to mount an attack on the Nanda empire. Conquering province after province of the empire with lightning rapidity, he finally attacked Magadha. The story of the war between Candragupta and the Nandas is preserved in several works, though no contemporary record has survived. One of the oldest of these works is the *Milindapañho* according to which the Nanda troops fought vigorously under the command of Bhaddasāla.[23] All the Nanda brothers perished in this war, though according to the *Mahāvaṁsa* the youngest of the Nandas, named Dhana Nanda, held out for some time after all his brothers were slain. With his death the family of the Nandas was exterminated. Candragupta's ally Parvataka died in the meanwhile, though the legends which relate to the manner of his death are contradictory and untrustworthy. Soon after he had redeemed the people of India by his glorious victories, Candragupta was crowned king[24] "over the whole of Jambudvīpa"[25] by his brāhmaṇa adviser Cāṇakya who became his prime minister.

The events which immediately followed the assumption of authority by Candragupta are related in the *Mudrārākṣasa*, a play which, though full of imaginary details, is probably based on events which actually occurred.[26] We learn from it that the son of Parvataka named Malayaketu rose against Candragupta with the help of five other chiefs and an ex-minister of King Nanda named Raksasa. The Machiavellian tactics of Cāṇakya, however, succeeded in sowing dissensions in the camp of Malayaketu, and the latter got his own allies murdered. By this act of his, Malayaketu was rendered powerless, and on the intervention of his friend, the ex-minister of Nanda, he was restored to his father's principality as a vassal of Candragupta.

The Maurya king at this time naturally became secure in his north Indian dominions. But his ambition of bringing the whole of his country under one sceptre was not yet fully realized. He pushed his conquests up to the western sea, for we learn from the Junagarh inscription of Rudradāman that Candragupta had control over Saurāṣṭra.[27] Candragupta also seems to have conquered a considerable portion of trans-Vindhyan India. According to Plutarch, Candragupta overran all India, which statement, even if we admit of exaggeration, means that Candragupta conquered the major portion of India.[28] This tradition is recorded in other documents also, for the *Mahāvaṁsa* says that Candragupta ruled over all Jambudvīpa.[29] According to Professor Aiyangar, Mulnamar, an ancient Tamil author, refers to the advance of Mauryas up to Tinnevelly district in early times.[30] Finally certain Mysore inscriptions refer to Candragupta's conquest of Mysore.[31] All these statements leave little room for doubt that Candragupta did conquer a considerable part of the Deccan.

Candragupta thus gained recognition as the paramount sovereign in the whole of India. He had, however, yet to measure strength with the greatest of his rivals, Seleucus Nicator, formerly a general of Alexander. Seleucus conquered Babylon in 312 BCE and soon made himself master of "the whole region from Phrygia to the Indus."[32] The river Indus also marked the north-western boundary of the Maurya empire at this time, and the two kings naturally came to blows. It is, however, surprising that the classical writers, who gave such minute details of Alexander's Indian campaigns, are so reticent in regard to the details of the conflict between Candragupta and Seleucus, and even the date of it is not known. It is, however, difficult to believe that Seleucus, having conquered the whole region from Phrygia to Indus, waited very long before trying to recover the Indian territory that had been conquered by Alexander. Seleucus, therefore, in all probability, crossed the Indus soon after becoming master of the region up to that river in 312 BCE and "waged war with Androkottos, King of the Indians, who dwelt on the banks of that stream." The fact that Candragupta was already present on the bank of the river Indus when Seleucus crossed that river probably means that the Maurya emperor was thinking of marching towards the western regions to emulate the legendary *digvijaya* of Māndhātṛ, Bharata, Raghu and other ancient kings. Thus the war between Candragupta and Seleucus was a clash between two ambitious kings. As we have already said, no details of the actual conflict are available, but the results as mentioned by the classical writers clearly show that Seleucus recognized the superiority of Candragupta and was obliged to conclude a humiliating treaty. According to this treaty, Seleucus gave a large part of Ariana to Candragupta in consequence of a marriage alliance. Dr. Smith has very ably shown[33] that the large part of Ariana referred to by Strabo[34] was identical with the former satrapies of Aria (Herat), Arachosia (Kandahar), Paropanisadiae (Kabul) and Gedrosia (Baluchistan) all of which Pliny considered as forming part of India.[35] As for the marriage contract, there is no reason to doubt its correctness because both Strabo and Appian refer to it. Thus the real explanation of the whole treaty seems to be that Seleucus married his daughter to Candragupta, giving the territories of Afghanistan and Baluchistan as a sort of dowry. The two royal families were in this way drawn on close friendly terms. We further learn that Candragupta presented 500 elephants to Seleucus and the latter sent an envoy named Megasthenes to the Indian court. Candragupta too must have sent an envoy to the Greek court, but his name is unfortunately not known.

Thus from a homeless wanderer five years before, Candragupta became the emperor of India and a large part of the former Persian empire. The war with Seleucus was in all probability the last war of Candragupta, and he devoted the remaining nineteen years of his reign in consolidating his empire and establishing a highly efficient system of administration. We can glance something of his personal life from the writings of Megasthenes preserved in fragments by other writers and, to some extent the *Arthaśāstra* of Kauṭilya, the name by which Cāṇakya is famous as an author.

Candragupta usually resided in the famous seat of his government, Pāṭaliputra, though occasionally he must have spent some time in other parts of his empire. The city of Pāṭaliputra was known to classical writers as Palibothra or Palimbothra and they have luckily preserved for us an account of this magnificent metropolis of the Mauryan empire. "The greatest city in India," we are told by Arrian, "is that which is called Palimbothra, in the dominions of the Prassians, where the streams of the Erannabaos (Hiraṇyavāha or what is now called Son) and the Ganges unite. It is eighty stadia (9 miles, 352 yards) in length and fifteen stadia (1 mile, 1270 yards) in breadth. It is of the shape of a parallelogram and is girded with a wooden wall pierced with loopholes for the discharges of arrows. Megasthenes informs us that "a ditch encompassed it all round which was six hundred feet in breadth and thirty cubits in depth and that the wall was crowned with 570 towers and had four and sixty gates."[36]

Candragupta lived in a very stately palace, containing gilded pillars adorned with golden vines and silver birds, and furnished with richly carved tables and chairs of state, as well as basins and goblets of gold. "In the Indian royal palace where the greatest of all the kings of the country resides, besides much else which is calculated to excite admiration and with which neither Susa nor Ekbatana can vie, there are other wonders besides. In the parks tame peacocks are kept, and pheasants which have been domes-ticated; there are shady groves and pasture grounds planted with trees, and branches which the art of the woodsman has deftly interwoven; while some trees are native to the soil, others are brought from other parts, and with their beauty enhance the charm of the landscape. Parrots are natives of the country and keep hovering about the king and wheeling round him, and vast though their numbers be, no Indian ever eats a parrot. The Brachmanes honour them highly above all other birds — because the parrot alone can imitate human speech. Within the palace grounds are artificial ponds in which they keep fish of enormous size but quite tame. No one has permission to fish for these except the king's sons while yet in their boyhood. These youngsters amuse themselves while fishing in the unruffled sheet of water, and learning how to sail their boats."[37]

Candragupta spent his leisure hours in the palace. The care of his person was entrusted to females who were armed.[38] He left his palace either for performing administrative duties or for offering sacrifices or for the chase. When he condescended to show himself in public, he was clothed in the finest muslin embroidered with purple and gold. When making short journeys, he rode on horseback, but when travelling longer distances, he was mounted on an elephant. The king did not sleep in the daytime. In the night he used to change his bedroom from time to time in order to defeat any plots against him.

Candragupta supervised the administration of justice himself. He did not allow the business to be interrupted even if he had to sit for the whole day, and the hour arrived when he had to attend to his person. In such a situation, he continued hearing cases, while four attendants massaged him with cylinders of wood.[39] His busy life seems to have been the cause of his abstaining from sleep during the daytime. Kauṭilya, in fact, lays down the precept that a king should so divide his timetable that he may not sleep for more than three hours.[40]

Along with his extraordinary devotion to duty, Candragupta also loved sports. He delighted in witnessing the fights of elephants, bulls, rams and rhinoceroses. A curious entertainment was provided by ox races. The most favourite sport was chase. The road along which he went for chase was marked with ropes and it was death to pass within the ropes. He shot arrows either from the back of an elephant or from a platform.[41]

From the fact that one of the occasions when the king left his palace was to offer sacrifices, it appears that Candragupta was a follower of the Vedic religion. According to the Jain tradition, he tilted towards Jainism during the last days of his life under the influence of the great Jain saint Bhadrabāhu. We learn from the *Rajāvalīkathe* that Candragupta became a Jain and having abdicated at the time of a great famine repaired with Bhadrabāhu to Mysore where he starved himself to death in the Jain fashion. In certain Mysore inscriptions dating from CE 900 the summit of the Kalbappu hill at Sravan Belgola is said to be marked with the footprints of the great *muni*s Bhadrabāhu and Candragupta.[42] The Jain tradition, however, is very confused with regard to details. Hemacandra, for example, does not speak of the retirement of Candragupta and Bhadrabāhu together to the southern direction. On the contrary, he suggests that Bhadrabāhu died in the sixteenth year of Candragupta's reign.[43] While there is no reason to doubt the Jain traditions that Candragupta in the last days of his life inclined towards Jainism as a result of his contact with the Jain saint Bhadrabāhu, it appears that the Candragupta who accompanied Bhadrabāhu to south India was different from the great Maurya emperor.

Candragupta led the life of an energetic emperor of a vast empire for 24 years. We do not know much about his family. His only son whose name is known to us under various forms was Bindusāra who succeeded him on the throne of Pāṭaliputra. If the Jain tradition is to be believed, the name of the mother of Bindusāra was Durdharā. It is a rather strange name for a lady and looks like the Sanskritization of some foreign name such as Diodora. Could it be the name of the Greek princess whom Candragupta married as one of the terms of his treaty with Seleucus?

Candragupta died in or about 293 BCE probably in his early fifties. The hard life that he led before he wore the crown of India and his extraordinary devotion to duty afterwards must have accelerated his death. But what he accomplished in this short span of life was really marvellous. By giving political unity to the greater part of India, he realized the age-long dream of the Indian people and for the first time in the long history of India earned the right to be called a *cakravartin*[44] and a *samrāṭ*.[45] He was not only great as a conqueror and an empire-builder, but was equally great as an organizer and administrator. It was the vigour and efficiency of the system of government which he had organized under the guidance of his wise chancellor Cāṇakya that kept the edifice of his empire practically unshaken[46] for more than a hundred years after his death.

Notes

1. Havell, *Aryan Rule in India*, p. 76.
2. *S.B.E.*, vol. XI, p. 134.
3. In the *Divyāvadāna* (p. 370) Bindusāra said to a woman, *tvam nāpinī aham rājā kṣatriyo mūrdhābhiṣiktaḥ, kathaṁ tvayā saha samāgamo bhaviṣyati*. In the same work (p. 409), Aśoka says to his queen Tiṣyarakṣitā, *devi aham kṣatriyaḥ kathaṁ palāṇḍuṁ paribhakṣayāmi*. These passages are significant.
4. *moriyānaṁ khattiyānaṁ vaṁse jātaṁ sirīdharaṁ*
   candaguttoti paññattaṁ caṇakko brāhmaṇo tato
   navamaṁ dhananandaṁ taṁ ghatetvā caṇḍakodhasā
   sakale jambudīpasmin rajje samabhisiñci so.
5. See Chapter 8, Section A.
6. *S.B.E.*, vol. XXXVI, p. 286.
7. "These 4 Kāṇva brāhmaṇas will enjoy the earth . . . ," Pargiter, *Dynasties of the Kali Age*, p. 71.
8. *Arthaśāstra*, VIII, 2.
9. *Ep. Ind.*, II, 222.

10. Rice, *Mysore and Coorg from Inscriptions*, 10.
11. *Annals and Antiquities of Rajasthan.*
12. The Moris were the ruling clan of Chittor till about CE 720 when their territory was wrested by a Guhilot king whom tradition calls by the name of Bappa.
13. Śrīdhara, the commentator of the *Viṣṇu Purāṇa*, and Ḍhunḍhirāja, the commentator of the *Mudrārākṣasa*, have invented the name Murā in their effort to give the etymology of the word Maurya, but the metronymic form Murā according to Sanskrit grammar will be Maureya, not Maurya.
14. The Mauryan monuments confirm the connection of the Mauryas with peacocks. For example, we find the figure of a peacock at the bottom of the Lauria Nandangarh pillar of Aśoka.
15. See Chapter 8, Section B.
16. See Chapter 8, Section D.
17. "Androkottos who was then but a youth saw Alexander etc."
18. Ḍhunḍhirāja's introduction to his commentary on the *Mudrārākṣasa*.
19. The name of Parvataka occurs in the *Pariśiṣṭaparvan*, the *Mahāvaṁsaṭīkā*, and the *Mudrārākṣasa*. Jacobi suggested the identification of this chief with a king of Nepal. F.W. Thomas has proposed his identification with Porus, but it cannot be accepted in view of the fact that Parvataka was, as his name shows, the ruler of some mountainous region, while the kingdom of Porus lay in the plains of the Punjab, east of the Jhelum.
20. Many scholars hold the view that the word 'Alexandrum' in Justin's account is a mistake for 'Nandrum' because according to Indian accounts, Candragupta offended Nanda and was obliged to flee.
21. See Chapter 8, Sections A and B.
22. See Chapter 8, Section D.
23. *S.B.E.*, vol. XXXVI, p. 147.
24. Coronation in Sanskrit is called *abhiṣeka* which literally means ablution. It is perhaps this ceremony which Strabo calls the hair-washing ceremony of the Indian king.
25. *Mahāvaṁsa*, V. In the Purāṇas, Jambudvīpa denotes the continent of which Bhārata forms a part, that is to say, what we now call Asia. But in the *Mahāvaṁsa*, as in many other works also, this term has

been used just as an appellation of India.

26. This is the opinion of Dr. Smith and Professor Hillebrandt.
27. See Appendix.
28. McCrindle, *Invasion of India by Alexander*, p. 310.
29. *Mahāvaṁsa*, V.
30. *Beginnings of South Indian History.*
31. Rice, *Mysore* and *Coorg from Inscriptions.*
32. Appian, *Roman History*, vol. II.
33. *Early History of India*, 4th ed., p. 158.
34. McCrindle, *Ancient India in Classical Literature*, pp. 15 and 88.
35. McCrindle, *Ancient India: Megasthenes and Arrian*, Fragm. LVI.
36. Ibid., Fragms. XXV and XXVI.
37. McCrindle, *Ancient India in Classical Literature*, pp. 141-42.
38. McCrindle, *Ancient India: Megasthenes and Arrian*, Fragm. XXVII; *Arthaśāstra*, I, 21.
39. Ibid., Fragm. XXVII. The celebrity of Candragupta's court is proved by Patañjali's reference to *Candraguptasabhā* in his *Mahābhāṣya* I, I, IX.
40. *Arthaśāstra* I, 20.
41. McCrindle, *Ancient India: Megasthenes and Arrian*, Fragm. XXVII.
42. Rice, *Epigraphia Carnatica*, vol. I, p. 31.
43. *Pariśiṣṭaparvan*, IX, 112.
44. The word *cakravartin* means a universal sovereign, and his *kṣetra* or sphere is defined in the *Arthaśāstra* of Kauṭilya (IX, I) as the whole of India extending from the Himālayas to the Indian Ocean and a thousand *yojanas* across.
45. According to the Purāṇas (*Vāyu* 45, 86; *Matsya* 114, 15), the king who conquers the whole of India is called a *samrāṭ* or emperor.
46. There is not even a shred of evidence in support of the assumption of some scholars that the Maurya empire was divided between Daśaratha and Samprati after the death of Aśoka.

4

Administration of the Empire

HAVING achieved the political unity of India, Candragupta applied all his energies in giving a good government to his people. Before, however, describing the system of administration prevalent in the reign of Candragupta, it is necessary to know the limits of his empire, which, though not known with absolute precision, can be approximately determined by combining the accounts of foreign writers with the Indian literary and epigraphic evidence.

The empire extended up to the borders of Persia in the north-west as gathered from the terms of the treaty with Seleucus Nicator. The whole of the Indo-Gangetic plain formed part of Candragupta's empire in which were probably also included the Himālayan states of Kashmir[1] and Nepal.[2] It extended in the west up to Kāṭhiāwār as is evident from the inscriptions of Rudradāman and in the east up to Bengal[3] which must have passed over to Candragupta from the Nandas who ruled over Gangaridae (Ganges delta) as well as Prassii (Prācī, i.e. Magadha).

Candragupta's empire included a large part of the trans-Vindhyan India also, as is clear from certain Mysore inscriptions and the statements of Plutarch and the Sri Lankan *Mahāvaṁsa* mentioned in Chapter 3. Tārānātha, however, represents Bindusāra as having conquered sixteen states which must have been situated in the south, because we know for certain that northern India was firmly held by Candragupta. It, therefore, means that either Candragupta was content to receive the submission of the kings of south India and it was left for Bindusāra to annex their territories or that what Bindusāra did was mostly the suppression of a general revolt. The latter view seems more tenable and thus there is nothing to invalidate the belief that Candragupta was the suzerain of a large portion of south India. Certain portions of this region, however, seem to have remained independent. The kingdom of Kaliṅga is described by Megasthenes as possessing considerable military force and was, no doubt, independent before its conquest by Aśoka.[4] The kingdom of Andhra which lay to its south is also described by Megasthenes as very powerful and it also might have been independent[5] in the time of Candragupta. The Pāṇḍya, Cola and Cera (Kerala) kingdoms of the extreme south were also left alone by Candragupta and his successors.[6] Thus Candragupta was the emperor of practically the whole subcontinent of India excluding Kaliṅga, Andhra and the Tamil land, but including Afghanistan and Baluchistan.

It should, however, be remembered that all this vast empire was not under the direct rule of Candragupta. There were protectorates as has always been the case in Indian history up to 1947. Kauṭilya lays down that "conquered kings preserved in their own lands in accordance with the policy of conciliation will be loyal to the conqueror and follow his sons and grandsons."[7] Literary and epigraphic evidence has preserved the names of at least two feudatory princes. The *Mudrārākṣasa* informs us that Malayaketu, the son of Parvataka, was allowed to rule his kingdom as a feudatory of Candragupta, while the Junagarh inscription of Rudradāman mentions the name of a Yavana vassal of Aśoka named Tuśāspha.[8] Kauṭilya mentions the names of certain *saṅgha*s or oligarchies like the Licchavis, the Vrajis, the Mallas, the Madras, the Kukuras, the Kurus, and the Pañcālas whose presidents or consuls were called *rājās*.[9] The territories of all of them except the Madras were included in the empire of the Nandas who seem to have allowed them a limited internal autonomy, and the same practice may have been followed by Candragupta. "The essence of this imperial system," in the words of Dr. Radha Kumud Mookerji, "was thus a recognition of local autonomy at the expense of the authority of the central government, which was physically unfit to assert itself except by its enforced affiliation to the pre-existing system of local government."[10]

We have ample material for describing the admi-nistration of the Maurya empire and Dr. Smith has rightly observed that "more is known about the policy of India as it was in the Maurya age than can be affirmed on the subject concerning any period intervening between that age and the reign of Akbar eighteen centuries later."[11] The chief source is the account left by the Greek ambassador Megasthenes. The *Arthaśāstra* of Kauṭilya tells us much about the methods of administration, many of which must have been followed by Candragupta, though the work seems to be largely theoretical. The edicts of Aśoka and even the Junagarh inscription of Rudradāman throw welcome light on the system of government prevalent in the reign of Candragupta.

The king was the head of the administration with absolute power and performed military, judicial, legislative and executive functions which we shall deal with as occasion arises. It should, however, be remembered that the power of the king was never unrestrained in ancient India[12] and Kauṭilya clearly lays down that "the king shall not consider as good that which pleases himself, but whatever pleases his subjects he shall consider as good."[13]

Kauṭilya mentions eighteen kinds of *amātyas* or high officials[14] who supervised all the branches of administration and were probably identical with the *mahāmātras* of Aśoka.

These officials were selected from men respected on account of their high character and wisdom and their appointment was the chief executive function of the king. As the detailed account of the administrative system will show, the measures taken by Chandragupta to promote the welfare and prosperity of his subjects do not support the stricture of Justin that "he suppressed with servitude the very people whom he had emancipated from foreign thraldom."[15]

Of the eighteen kinds of *amātyas* mentioned by Kauṭilya, the highest were the *mantrin* or chancellor, the *purohita* or high priest, the *senāpati* or commander-in-chief of the army and the *yuvarāja* or crown prince. Each of them got a salary of 48,000 *paṇas*[16] per annum. They formed a sort of inner cabinet of the king in accordance with the precept of Kauṭilya that the confidential advisors of the king should not be less than three and more than four.[17]

The second category of high officials were the *dauvārika* or the chief reception officer of the king, the *antarvaṁśika* or the chief officer-in-charge of the royal harem, the *praśāstṛ* or the chief information officer, the *sannidhātṛ* or chamberlain and the *samāhartṛ* or collector-general, each of whom got a salary of 24,000 *paṇas* per annum. The duty of the *dauvārika* was to fix the time for and explain the proper etiquette to those seeking audience with the king. The *antarvaṁśika* looked after the needs and comforts of the inmates of the royal harem. The *praśāstṛ* wrote and transmitted the orders of the king. The *sannidhātṛ* was both a chamberlain and a treasurer. He had charge of the construction of treasuries and warehouses wherever they were required and was the custodian of the realized revenue in cash and kind. He had also the duties of constructing armouries, courts of justice and offices of ministers and secretaries. The *samāhartṛ* was the officer who supervised the collection of revenue from the whole kingdom. He was assisted in his work by the *gopa* who had the charge of five to ten villages and the *sthānika* who was higher than *gopa* and had the charge of a whole district.

The third category of high officials were the members of the *mantripariṣad*, the *pauravyāvahārika* or the city magistrate, the *rāṣṭrapāla* or governor of a province, the *antapāla* or officer-in-charge of the borders, the *karmāntika* or the officer-in-charge of state manufactories and the *nāyaka* or the chief of police, each of whom got a salary of 12,000 *paṇa*s per anum. The *mantripariṣad* appears to have been, as rightly observed by Dr. D.R. Bhandarkar, a body corresponding to the modern secretariats. It formed a kind of link between the king and his high officials. Their duty was to start the work that had not yet begun, to complete what had begun, to improve what had been accomplished and to enforce strict obedience to orders.[18] The *pauravyāvahārika*, who was no doubt the same as the *nagaravyāvahārika* of Aśoka's inscriptions, administered justice in the city in his charge. The head of the government of one of the provinces of the different zones into which the empire must have been divided was called *rāṣṭrapāla* or governor. The *antapāla* was guardian of the borders, and one of his duties according to the inscriptions of Aśoka was to look after the welfare and improvement of the condition of the wild tribes dwelling in some parts of the borders. The state employed many artisans and the *karmāntika* was probably the officer-in-charge of them. The *nāyaka* was probably the chief of the police force of a province.

To the fourth category of high officials belonged the *pradeṣṭṛ* or district officers, the *śreṇimukhya*s or heads of the trade guilds, and the *mukhya*s or the chiefs of the four wings of the army, each of whom received 8,000 *paṇa*s per annum. The duty of the *pradeṣṭṛ*, besides acting as a link between the *samāhartṛ* and the *sthānika* for the collection of revenue, was also to administer criminal justice (*kaṇṭakaśodhana*). The *śreṇīmukhya*s were probably heads of the guilds of artisans or merchants.

The *mukhyas* of the different wings of the army, judging from their salary, were probably captains of a battalion or regiment of any of the wings of the army.

Besides the high officials mentioned above, there were a host of other officers like the *vanapāla* or forest officer and the *adhyakṣas* or the heads of various departments. There was a network of spies to test the purity of officials.

Kauṭilya recognizes three kinds of envoys.[19] The envoy who was sent to a foreign country with full powers was called a *nisṛṣṭārtha* or an ambassador. The envoy who was sent with limited powers was called a *parimitārtha* or chargé d'-affaires. The third kind of envoy was only the conveyor of some royal writ and was called a *śāsanahara*.

It is clear from the description of these officials and of the various *adhyakṣas* in Book II of the *Arthaśāstra*, that there was an all-pervading and highly efficient bureaucracy in the Mauryan empire. No doubt the *Arthaśāstra* was written as a *śāstra* probably before the foundation of the Maurya empire, but since its author Kauṭilya became the prime minister of the empire, he must have implemented many of the ideas of his own book. We can discern several similarities between the practices of the Mauryan and Hellenistic monarchies, which is natural on account of their close contact and the similarity of problems they had to face. But as Dr. Nilakanta Sastri has rightly pointed out, "both were aided by models set by the empire of the Achaemenids," for "the administrative machinery of Alexander and his successors was virtually a continuation of that of the Persian monarchs."[20]

We can describe the administration of the empire of Candragupta under six heads, namely (1) Military administration, (2) Municipal administration, (3) Village administration, (4) Provinces, (5) Finance and (6) Law and Justice.

The military administration of the Mauryan empire was very elaborate and efficient. The Mauryas maintained a large standing army drawing regular pay and supplied by the government with arms and equipment. Pliny, no doubt on the authority of Megasthenes, put the strength of Candragupta's army at 600,000 infantry, 30,000 cavalry and 9,000 elephants. He says nothing about chariots. The Nandas, who were the immediate predecessors of Candragupta possessed 8,000 chariots according to the highest estimate, and the number in possession of Candragupta may be assumed to be at least the same. Each elephant carried four men including the driver, and each chariot carried three men including the driver. Thus the number of men with elephants and chariots was 36,000 and 24,000 respectively. The total number of men in the army of Candragupta according to these figures was 690,000. There must have been a large number of cantonments in the whole empire.

The highest officer in the army was the *senāpati* or the commander-in-chief and he must have led the army to suppress rebellions. It should, however, be remembered that the military function was one of the four main functions of the king and, as Megasthenes informs us, he left his palace to lead the army himself in the time of war.[21]

We learn from Megasthenes that there was a regular war office for military administration. There was a commission of 30 members divided into six boards each consisting of five members.[22] Kauṭilya seems to refer to these very boards when he says that the departments looking after the needs of the four wings of the army "shall each be officered with many chiefs."[23]

The first board was in charge of navy, and worked in cooperation with the admiral who was probably identical with the *nāvadhyakṣa* of the *Arthaśāstra*. This officer performed all the duties relating to the ships such as hiring of ships to passengers, collecting toll from merchants, arrest of suspicious persons, and destruction of *himsrikas* or pirates.[24] The ships were maintained by the state and were not restricted to rivers but ventured to the sea. These regulations clearly show that there was a considerable ocean traffic in Mauryan times.

The second board was in charge of transport, com-missariat, and army service, and worked in cooperation with the superintendent of bullock trains who was probably identical with the *godhyakṣa* of the *Arthaśāstra*.[25] The bullock trains were used for transporting engines of war, food for the soldiers, provender for cattle, and other military requisites.

The third board was in charge of infantry and probably worked in co-operation with the *pattyadhyakṣa* mentioned in the *Arthaśāstra*.[26] Arrian has preserved an account of the way in which the Indian foot-soliders equipped themselves for war:

"The foot soldiers," we are told, "carry a bow made of equal length with the man who bears it. This they rest upon the ground and pressing against it with their left foot thus discharge the arrow, having drawn the string far backwards: for the shaft they use is little short of being three yards long and there is nothing which can resist an Indian archer's shot, neither shield nor breastplate nor any stronger defence, if such there be. In their left hand they carry bucklers made of undressed ox hide, which are not so broad as those who carry them, but are about as long. Some are equipped with javelins instead of bows, but all wear a sword which is broad in the blade, but not longer than three cubits, and this, when they engage in close fight they wield with both hands to fetch down a lustier blow."[27]

The fourth board was in charge of cavalry and probably worked in co-operation with the *Aśvādhyakṣa* mentioned in the *Arthaśāstra*.[28] Each horseman was equipped with two lances and a shorter buckler than that carried by the foot-soldiers.[29]

The horses of Kāmboja and Sindhu were regarded as the best.[30]

The fifth and sixth boards were in charge of the war elephants and the war chariots respectively. Kauṭilya calls the superintendents of the elephants and the chariots as the *hastyadhyakṣa*[31] and the *rathādhyakṣa*[32] respectively.

There were royal stables for the horses and the elephants and also a royal magazine for the arms, because the solider had to return his arms to the magazine and his horse and his elephant to the stables.[33]

The civil administration of Candragupta was equally efficient. The method of urban administration prevailing at that time may first be described. According to the *Arthaśāstra*, the administration of the towns was carried on by the *nāgaraka* or town officer with the assistance of the *sthānika*s and the *gopa*s. Each *gopa* had charge of the details of a fixed number of families in the town and the *sthānika* supervised their work.[34] This system of administration, if actually prevalent, must have been applicable to small towns. For a knowledge of the system of administration prevailing in big cities, we must turn to Megasthenes who has left an account of the way in which Pāṭaliputra, the capital, was governed. Other metropolitan cities of the empire, such as Taxila and Ujjain must have been governed on the same lines.

There was a regular municipal commission, which also consisted of six boards, each composed of five members.[35] Kauṭilya also mentions some *adhyakṣa*s or superintendents whose duties exactly correspond to the functions of the boards referred to above. Thus the *pautavādhyakṣa*[36] or the superintendent of weights and measures, the *paṇyādhyakṣa*[37] or the superintendent of trade, and the *śulkādhyakṣa*[38] or the superintendent of tolls had duties similar to those assigned to the last three boards by Megasthenes. It is, therefore, probable that every board worked in co-operation with a superintendent as in the case of military administration. Much of the administrative elaboration noticed by the Greeks, however, must have been due to the genius of Candragupta.

The first board looked after everything relating to industrial arts. Its members appear to have been responsible for fixing the rates of wages as well as supervising the works which the artisans did. Artisans were regarded as servants of state, and anybody who rendered an artisan incapable of work by causing the loss of his eyes or hands was sentenced to capital punishment.[39]

The second board was responsible for watching the foreigners and attending to their requirements. This board provided the foreigners lodging and escorts and, in case of need, medical attendance. If any foreigner died he was decently buried, and his property was handed over to the rightful claimant. These regulations clearly prove that Candragupta created widespread political and commercial relations with foreign powers to necessitate such administration.

The third board was in charge of vital statistics. All births and deaths were systematically registered, not only to facilitate the collection of taxes, but also for the information of the government. The high value attached to statistics by the Maurya government has justly evoked the wonder and admiration of modern scholars.

The fourth board supervised commerce, and was authorized to enforce the use of duly stamped weights and measures. A merchant could deal only in one commodity, for which licence was given, unless he had paid a double licence tax.

The fifth board was required to supervise the trade of manufactured articles. New and old goods were required to be sold separately, and there was a fine for mixing the two. It appears from the *Arthaśāstra* that old things could be sold only by special permission.[40]

The sixth board collected tithes on sales, the rate being one-tenth of the profit. If anyone practised fraud in the payment of this tax, his punishment was death, probably when the amount involved was large.[41] It, however, appears that the evasion of this tax for honest reasons was not so treated. Even then the penalty was very severe according to modern standards.[42]

In their collective capacity the members of the municipal commission were responsible for the general administration of the city and for keeping the markets, temples, harbours and other public works of the city in order.

The rural administration of the Mauryan empire may best be described in the words of Megasthenes:

> Of the great officers of state some superintend the rivers, measure land, as is done in Egypt, and inspect the sluices by which water is let out from the main canals into their branches, so that every one may have an equal supply of it. The same persons have charge also of huntsmen and are entrusted with the power of rewarding or punishing them according to their deserts. They collect the taxes, and superintend the occupations connected with land as those of the woodcutters, the carpenters, the blacksmiths and the miners. They construct roads and at every ten stadia set up a pillar to show the by roads and distances."[43]

These regulations show the exceedingly progressive outlook of the Maurya government. The excellent main-tenance of roads is evidence of the importance attached by the Maurya government to proper communication between different parts of the empire. The regulations about forests, mines, agriculture, and irrigation deserve to be noticed in some detail.

Forests have always been a great asset for human beings. They not only supply wood, but are also necessary for a good environment. The Maurya government fully realized their importance. The statement of Megasthenes according to which one of the great officers of state supervised the occupations of woodcutters and carpenters connected with forest is supported by the *Arthaśāstra* which mentions an officer called *vanapāla*[44] who was in charge of the forests and who must have supervised the occupations connected with them.

Mining and metallurgy are indispensable for the industrial growth of a country, and the Maurya government was not oblivious of this fact. The statement of Megasthenes in this respect too finds support from Kauṭilya who regards mines as the source of treasury and mentions a special officer of mining called the *ākāradhyakṣa*.[45] This officer must have assisted the great officers mentioned by Megasthenes.

Agriculture has always been the main industry of India and so it was in the days of the Maurya empire. The Maurya emperors did everything to promote agriculture, and according to the *Arthaśāstra* there was a special officer in charge of agriculture called the *sītādhyakṣa*[46] who must have assisted the great officers mentioned by Megasthenes. Of the various measures taken by the Maurya government for the benefit of farmers, one was the system of rewarding and punishing the huntsmen. The role of these huntsmen is explained by Megasthenes in another context as follows: "By hunting and trapping they clear the country of noxious birds and wild beasts. As they apply themselves eagerly and assiduously to this pursuit, they free India from the pests with which it abounds — all sorts of wild beasts and birds which devour the seeds sown by the husbandmen."[47] Megasthenes further informs us that "There are usages observed by the Indians which contribute to prevent the occurrence of famine among them;

for whereas among other nations it is usual in the context of war to ravage soil and thus to reduce it to an uncultivated waste, among the Indians, on the contrary, by whom husbandmen are regarded as a class that is sacred and inviolable, the tillers of the soil, even when battle is raging in their neighbourhood are undisturbed by any sense of danger, for the combatants on either side in waging the conflict make carnage of each other, but allow those engaged in husbandry to remain quite unmolested."[48] When famine did occur, the state promulgated various relief measures which will be described in the next chapter.

An important auxiliary of agriculture is irrigation, which also received the full attention of the Maurya government according to Megasthenes. Luckily we have epigraphic evidence to prove the efficiency of the Maurya government in providing the facility of irrigation to the people of even the remotest provinces of the empire. The Junagarh inscription of the Śaka satrap Rudradāman engraved about the year CE 150 tells us something about the history of the Lake Beautiful (Sudarśana) of Kāṭhiāwār.[49] We are told that Puṣyagupta, the Vaiśya, who was the governor of Surāṣṭra in the reign of Candragupta Maurya, noticing the needs of local farmers, dammed up a small stream and thus provided a reservoir of great value. It was adorned with conduits in the time of Candragupta's grandson Aśoka. This work endured for four hundred years, until in CE 150, a storm of a "most tremendous fury befitting the end of a mundane period" destroyed the embankment.

Keeping the efficiency of administration in view, the empire was divided into four zones, each zone being subdivided into a number of provinces. Besides the home provinces of eastern India, which appear to have been under the direct control of the emperor, there were at least three viceroyalties as can be inferred from the edicts of Aśoka. The viceroy of the north-western provinces had his headquarters at Taxila from where he seems to have controlled Afghanistan, Baluchistan, the Punjab, Kashmir and Sindh. The viceroy of western India was stationed at Ujjain and controlled Mālwā and Gujarat. The viceroy of south had his capital at Suvarṇagiri, which was probably situated in the Raichur district[50] of what is now the state of Karnataka. The viceroys of these territories were styled Kumāras[51] or Āryaputras and were princes of royal blood. Each of the four zones was divided into a number of provinces. The administrative head of a province was called *rāṣṭrapāla* or governor. From the Junagarh inscription we know the name of one such governor of Candragupta's time, the Vaiśya Puṣyagupta who governed the province of Surāṣṭra and is called its *rāṣṭrya,* no doubt the same as the *rāṣṭrapāla* of the *Arthaśāstra.* Like the Mughal emperor Akbar and his successors at a much later period, the Maurya emperors appointed their feudatory princes as governors of the provinces of their empire. It appears that there were some Yavana or Greek feudatory princes in the north-western zone of the empire and one of them Tuṣāspha was appointed governor of Surāṣṭra by Aśoka.

It was recognized that "all undertakings depend upon finance."[52] The *samāhartṛ* or collector-general supervised the collection of dues from various sources. The mainstay of finance was, no doubt, land revenue. The normal share of the crown recognized by Hindu lawgivers was 1/6 of the gross produce[53] which is also referred to by Kauṭilya at one place.[54] Diodorus, however, mentions the share of the government as having been 1/4 of the gross produce. The fact seems to be that in practice the proportion varied largely depending on the economic condition, fertility of the soil, etc. of the different parts of the empire.

The other sources of revenue as listed by Kauṭilya were: (1) other dues and cesses laid on land including a water rate, (2) tax on houses in towns, (3) income from forests and mines, (4) customs at the frontiers, octroi at the city gate, tolls and ferry dues and road taxes, (5) fees for licences of various kinds to be taken out by artisans, craftsmen, professionals and traders, (6) fines levied in law courts and (7) ownerless property. We learn from Patañjali that the Mauryas introduced the worship of images with a view to obtain gold.[55] This perhaps means that the government erected temples with images in them and the offerings made by the devotees before the images in cash and kind went to the government. In times of national emergency benevolences (*praṇaya*) were resorted to and the rich were compelled to give some part of their wealth to the state.

The main items of expenditure were: (1) the maintenance of the king and his court and of the members 2of the royal family befitting their dignity, (2) the salaries of various high and low officials, (3) expenditure on the army including salaries and equipment, (4) public works like buildings of various kinds, roads, irrigation work, the erection of forts and arsenals and their proper equipment, (5) the maintenance of the families of soldiers and civil officials dying in state service, (6) the care of the unemployed and the indigent, (7) compensation for theft, (8) outlay on industrial, mining and other enterprises undertaken by the state, (9) payment to skilled artisans who were regarded as servants of the state, and (10) grants to religious institutions of various kinds.

The bureaucracy was assisted by an organized system of espionage. The system of espionage has always been hated by people and so it must have been in the days of Candragupta. But it had its good points also. It was recognized by Indian statesmen that a king should not rule against the wishes of his subjects. So the spies were employed not only to detect criminals, but also to get information about the views of the people. An unpleasing feature of the espionage system was that even courtesans were utilized for this purpose.[56] Arrian says that the reports which these spies gave were always true, for no Indian could be accused of lying.[57] This statement is not in contradiction with other records of the character of ancient Indians, though its strict accuracy may be doubted.

Megasthenes erroneously asserts that there was no written law in India. As a matter of fact sacred writings were one of the four legs of law, the other three according to Kauṭilya being custom, agreement, and the edicts of the king,[58] the issuing of which from time to time constituted the legislative function of the king. Of these four legs, whenever there was conflict between custom and sacred law or between agreement and sacred law, the sacred law overrode the other two.[59] But when sacred law was in conflict with rational law, then reason or rational law was held authoritative.[60] Since the king's edicts were issued in consultation with the wisest men of the state, they were taken as rational law, and hence in enumerating the four legs of law as sacred writings, agreement, custom and edicts of the king, Kauṭilya clearly says that the last (*paścimaḥ*) is superior to the first three (*pūrva*).[61] This is, no doubt, a bold statement and is found only in *Nārada* among later texts. There is, however, no evidence to support the view that Kauṭilya was influenced by contemporary foreign practice when he put forward this new principle in his work.[62]

The administration of justice was carried on by two sets of state courts, though in the first instance some of the disputes must have been dealt with by village *panchāyat*s and tribunals appointed by clans, guilds and corporations.[63] The two sets of state courts were styled *dharmasthīya* and *kaṇṭakaśodhana* respectively and corresponded roughly to the modern civil and criminal courts. They were established at headquarters called *janapadasandhi, saṅgrahaṇa, droṇamukha* and *sthānīya* with jurisdiction over two, ten, four hundred and eight hundred villages respectively. The *dharmasthīya* courts were presided over by three *dharmastha*s (judges learned in sacred law) and three *amātyas* (high officials proficient in jurisprudence).[64] The main heads of civil law were: (1) marriage and the property of women, (2) inheritance, (3) disputes over the sale, boundaries and other matters concerning houses, (4) debt, (5) deposits, (6) slaves, (7) labour and contract, (8) sale and purchase, (9) violence, (10) defamation, (11) assault, and (12) gambling. In many respects Kauṭilya is more rational and liberal than the authors of the ancient texts on sacred law and the actual Mauryan system of justice must have been influenced by his ideas.

The *kaṇṭakaśodhana* (removal of thorns) courts were presided over by three *pradeṣṭṛs* and three *amātyas*.[65] The aim of these courts appears to have been the protection of the state and people from the baneful actions of anti-social persons who were regarded as the thorns of the society. Theft, murder, burglary, rape, the use of false weights and measures, bribery and treason against the king were some of the offences brought before these courts. On the one hand, these courts protected the interests of the artisans against those prone to harm them, and, on the other hand, the interests of the consumers against any cheating on the part of the artisans and the merchants. The use of spies for the detection of criminals was also resorted to be these courts.

Each set of courts had a hierarchical order. The case decided by a lower court could proceed to a higher court if the parties were dissastisfied. The final authority lay with the king, and we know from Megasthenes that a large number of people sought the intervention of the king in deciding their cases.[66] The decision of such cases as had not been satisfactorily decided by the courts constituted the judicial function of the king.

The procedure of the law courts was equally interesting. The plaintiff had to file the suit along with the name and date, and the defendant had similarly to give his reply in writing. Witnesses as well as documentary evidence were recognized. Certain agreements, such as those entered into in seclusion, in the dead of night or with fraud, were held void.[67]

The penal code was simple. Offences were generally punished with fines, there being three kinds of the latter, viz. the first amercement ranging up to 96 *paṇa*s, the middlemost amercement ranging up to 500 *paṇa*s, and the highest amercement ranging up to 1000 *paṇa*s.[68] Crimes which surpassed those for which the highest amercement was prescribed, were punishable with *vadha*, which term, according to ancient authorities, meant corporal chas-tisement including beating, shaving off of the hair, imprisonment, mutilation and death.[69] These crimes were generally those which involved violence or moral turpitude, such as murder, rape, hurt, theft, fraud and the submission of false evidence. Even in some of these crimes there were grades. Thus a thief who stole a property up to the value of 50 *paṇa*s was punishable with the highest amercement, but if he stole goods worth more than 50 *paṇa*s, he was punished with *vadha* or corporal chastisement, which extended up to death, if the offense was very serious.[70] Those persons who spoke a lie, that is to say committed fraud in the payment of tolls, were also punished like thieves.[71] Injury to the limb of any person was punished with the mutilation of the corresponding limb as well as a hand, and if the person injured happened to be an artisan, the punishment was death.[72] Judicial torture was also recognized as a method of eliciting confession, but it was used with the greatest caution.[73] The efficiency of criminal administration is attested to by Megasthenes who says that in a population of 400,000 men (and women) in Pāṭaliputra, the thefts recorded on any one day did not exceed the value of two hundred drachmae or about eight pounds sterling.[74] Kauṭilya lays down, in agreement with the *Dharmaśāstra*s, that "whatever of the property of citizens robbed by thieves the king cannot recover shall be made good from his own pocket."[75]

On certain occasions prisoners were set free. One such occasion was the birthday of the King. Other occasions are enumerated by Kauṭilya in the following passage: "Whenever a new country is conquered, when an heir apparent is installed on the throne, or when a prince is born to the king, prisoners are usually set free."[76]

Notes

1. Kalhaṇa mentions Aśoka among the kings of Kashmir, but as Aśoka is known to have conquered only Kaliṅga, we may conclude that Kashmir already formed part of the empire of Bindusāra and probably also of Candragupta. The *Mudrārākṣasa* play mentions the prince of Kashmir among the subordinate allies of Malayaketu who subsequently became a vassal of Candragupta.
2. Aśoka's inscribed pillars at Rummindei and Nigalisagar and the Nepalese tradition attributing the foundation of the city of Patan near Kathmandu to Aśoka prove the inclusion of Nepal in his empire and probably also of his father and grandfather.
3. The discovery in 1931 of the Mahāsthān inscription written in the Brāhmī script of the Mauryan epoch further confirms the inclusion of Bengal in the Maurya empire. There is no evidence for or against the inclusion of Assam in the Maurya empire.
4. "The royal city of Calingae is called Parthalis. Over their king 60,000 foot soldiers, 1,000 horsemen, 700 elephants keep watch and ward in 'precinct of war.'" McCrindle, *Ancient India: Megasthenes and Arrian*, Fragm. LVI (22).
5. "Next came the Andrae, a still more powerful race, which possesses numerous villages and thirty towns defended by walls and towers, and which supplies its king with an army of 100,000 infantry, 2,000 cavalry and 1,000 elephants." McCrindle, *Ancient India: Megasthenes and Arrian*, Fragm. LVI (22).
6. Aśoka mentions these kingdoms as independent in his edicts.
7. *Arthaśāstra*, VII, 16.
8. Megasthenes mentions several petty principalities ruled by their own 'kings' but it is difficult to identify most of them.

9. *Arthaśāstra*, XI, 1.
10. Dr. Radha Kumud Mookerji, *Local Government in Ancient India*, p. 10.
11. Dr. V.A. Smith, *Aśoka — the Buddhist Emperor of India*, p. 84.
12. In the Vedic age the power of the king was restrained by two popular assemblies known as the *Sabhā* and the *Samiti*. The Pauras and Jānapadas mentioned in the epics were also according to K.P. Jayaswal (*Hindu Polity*, pp. 70-108) really popular assemblies representing citizens and villagers and had considerable powers.
13. *Arthaśāstra*, I, 19.
14. Ibid., I, 12.
15. See Chapter 8, Section D.
16. *Arthaśāstra* V, 3. A *paṇa* was equivalent to eighty cowries. The value of a *paṇa* according to Dr. Smith (*Early History of India*, 149), was not far from a shilling.
17. *Arthaśāstra*, I, 15.
18. Ibid.
19. Ibid., I, 16.
20. *Age of the Nandas and Mauryas*, 178.
21. McCrindle, *Ancient India: Megasthenes and Arrian*, Fragm. XXVI.
22. Ibid, Fragm. XXXIV.
23. *Arthaśāstra*, II, 4.
24. Ibid., II, 28.
25. Ibid., II, 29.
26. Ibid., II, 33.
27. McCrindle, *Ancient India : Megasthenes and Arrian, Indika of Arrian*, XVI.
28. *Arthaśāstra*, II, 30.
29. McCrindle, *Ancient India : Megasthenes and Arrian, Indika of Arrian*, XVI.
30. *Arthaśāstra*, II, 30.
31. Ibid., II, 31.
32. Ibid., II, 33.
33. McCrindle, *Ancient India : Megasthenes and Arrian*, Fragm. XXXIV.
34. *Arthaśāstra* II, 36.

35. McCrindle, *Ancient India : Megasthenes and Arrian*, Fragm. XXXIV.
36. *Arthaśāstra* II, 19.
37. Ibid., II, 16.
38. Ibid., II, 21.
39. McCrindle, *Ancient India : Megasthenes and Arrian*, Fragm. XXVII.
40. *Arthaśāstra*, IV, 2.
41. This regulation appears to be identical with that given by Kauṭilya in connection with the payments of tolls, viz. "Those who utter a lie shall be punished as thieves" (*Arthaśāstra*, II, 21). If this is so, then fraud involving a large amount only must have been punished by death, as in the case of theft. The words of Kauṭilya clearly prove that evasion of taxes by dishonest means alone was punishable.
42. It may be mentioned here that as late as the eighteenth century forgery was a capital offence in English law.
43. McCrindle, *Ancient India : Megasthenes and Arrian*, Fragm. XXXIV. Ten stadia must have been equivalent to some Indian measure of distance, probably half a *kos* (or about one mile).
44. *Arthaśāstra*, V, 3.
45. Ibid., II, 12.
46. Ibid., II, 24.
47. McCrindle, *Ancient India : Megasthenes and Arrian*, Fragm. I (40).
48. Ibid., Fragm. I (36).
49. Vide Appendix.
50. Smith, *Aśoka*, p. 91n.
51. The word Kumāra in *Arthaśāstra*, V, 3, is used in the sense of a minor prince, as is evident from the fact that it is immediately followed by the word Kumāramātṛ which Dr. Shamasastry has correctly translated as "the nurse of the prince."
52. *Arthaśāstra*, II, 8.
53. *Manu*, 7, 130; *Yājñavalkya*, I, 13, 335.
54. *Arthaśāstra*, I, 13.
55. *Mauryair hiraṇyārthibhir arcāḥ prakalpitāḥ*.
56. McCrindle, *Ancient India*: *Megasthenes and Arrian*, Fragm. XXXIII; *Arthaśāstra* II, 27.
57. Ibid., *Indika of Arrian*, XII.
58. *Arthaśāstra*, III, 1, 51.

59. Ibid., III, 1, 56.

60. Ibid., III, 1, 57.

61. Dr. Shamasastry's translation of III, 1, 51 (last line) as "Of these four, in order, the latter is superior to the one previously named" is inaccurate, because in verse 56 of this very chapter Kauṭilya clearly declares sacred writings as superior to both agreement and custom.

62. K.A. Nilakanta Sastri, *Age of the Nandas and Mauryas*, p. 175.

63. *Yājñavalkya*, II, 2, 30.

64. *Arthaśāstra*, III, 1. The *janapadasandhi* court seems to have had jurisdiction over two villages and not two districts as held by Shamasastry, because the order of enumeration suggests that it was the lowest court.

65. *Arthaśāstra*, IV, 1.

66. McCrindle, *Ancient India*: *Megasthenes and Arrian*, Fragm. XXVII.

67. *Arthaśāstra*, III, 1.

68. Ibid., III, 17.

69. *Vadha* is unanimously interpreted by ancient commentators as corporal punishment, not necessarily death. Manu and other ancient lawgivers recognize four kinds of punishment, namely *Vāgdaṇḍa* or warning, *dhigdaṇḍa* or scolding, *dhanadaṇḍa* or fine and finally *vadhadaṇḍa* which is explained by Kullūka, Vijñāneśvara and others as corporal punishment from beating and imprisonment to death (*Manu*, 8, 129, *Yājña*, 1, 13, 367). Kauṭilya several times jumps from trifling fines to *vadha* and it would be absurd to maintain that he has reserved the meaning of that term for death.

70. *Arthaśāstra*, IV, 9.

71. *Arthaśāstra*, II, 21; McCrindle, *Ancient India*: *Megasthenes and Arrian*, Fragm. XXXIV.

72. Ibid., Fragm. XXVII.

73. *Arthaśāstra*, IV, 8. Kauṭilya expressly says that "the production of conclusive evidence shall be insisted upon," and to defend his opinion he gives the example of a certain Māṇḍavya, who, though innocent, "confessed" when tortured.

74. McCrindle, *Ancient India* : *Megasthenes and Arrian*, Fragm. XXVIII.

75. *Arthaśāstra*, III, 16.

76. Ibid., II, 36.

5

Religious, Social and Economic Conditions

No account of the life story of a monarch can be said to be complete without a description of the beliefs and the practices, the manners and the customs, and the vocations and the callings of the people over whom he ruled. We have fortunately enough material, both literary and epigraphic, with the help of which a good account of the religious, social and economic life of the period can be given.

India is the birthplace of many religions. The seventh pillar edict of Aśoka gives some information about the religions of the Maurya period when it mentions the *Saṅgha* (the Buddhist church), the Brāhmaṇas, the *Nirgrantha*s and the *Ājīvika*s as the four religious orders of his time. The mentions of the *Saṅgha* and the Brāhmaṇas, no doubt, indicates the prevalence of Buddhism and the Vedic religion respectively. The *Nirgrantha*s were the Jains, and the *Ājīvika*s were the followers of an ascetic sect now long extinct.

Of these the Vedic religion was the most ancient and the most widely prevalent in the time of Candragupta Maurya. With the passage of long centuries it had come to be divided into three branches which may be called ritualistic, philosophical, and theistic respectively. They were, however, not totally exclusive of each other.

The characteristic feature of the first of these branches of the Vedic religion, which laid stress on *karma* or ritual, was the performance of *yajñas* or sacrifices to Indra, Varuṇa, Agni and other Vedic deities. The Brāhmaṇical *Śrautasūtras*, the Buddhist Canonical texts, and the account of Megasthenes, all bear testimony to the widely prevalent cult of sacrifices. Besides the *aśvamedha* and the *rājasūya* sacrifices meant only for kings, there were fourteen other sacrifices known as the *śrauta yajñas*. Seven of these were called *haviryajñas*, the best known of which was the *agnihotra*, while the other seven were called *soma yajñas*, the best known of which was the *vājapeya*. Many of these *yajñas* entailed the immolation of animals. Most of these sacrifices were, however, confined to kings, nobles, wealthy brāhmaṇas and rich businessmen who formed the aristocratic class of the time. These sacrifices required at least four priests, while in some of them there were as many as sixteen priests. These priests who formed a section of the brāhmaṇa caste, were adept in the ritual of sacrifices and got rich fees from their patrons. The prevalence of the sacrificial aspect of the Vedic religion among persons of the aristocratic class in the Mauryan period is proved by the testimony of Megasthenes. Mentioning the brāhmaṇa priests as philosophers, Megasthenes informs us that they were engaged by private persons to offer sacrifices and that in requital of such services they received valuable gifts and privileges.[1] We further learn from Megasthenes that one of the occasions when Candragupta left his palace was to offer sacrifice.[2]

The second branch of Vedic religion in which stress was laid on *jñāna* or spiritual knowledge was based on the teachings of the *Upaniṣads*. It appealed to the intellectuals of those times. The leaders of this school of thought were those brāhmaṇas who, in accordance with the precept of the *Kaṭha Upaniṣad*, preferred the *śreya* or good to the *preya* or pleasing. These brāhmaṇas lived up to the ideal of plain living and high thinking and did not have much interest in the Vedic sacrifices. Even Kauṭilya, the mentor of Candragupta, does not seem to have been very enthusiastic about the performance of sacrifices. Had he really been inclined that way, he would surely have persuaded Candragupta to perform the horse sacrifice (*aśvamedha*) for which no other Indian king ever was more qualified than the mighty Maurya monarch. The best account of these brāhmaṇas is furnished by Megasthenes, who has written on the basis of his personal observation.

Megasthenes speaks about two kinds of Indian philosophers known as the Brachmanes and the Sarmanes. The Brachmanes were no doubt the brāhmaṇas. Regarding their views on creation and allied matters, this is what he says: "On many points their opinions coincide with those of the Greeks, for like them they say that the world had a beginning and is liable to destruction, and is in shape spherical, and that the Deity who made it and who governs it is diffused through all its parts. They hold that various first principles operate in the universe, and that water was the principle employed in the making of the world. In addition to the four elements there is a fifth agency (the ether or sky) from which the heaven and the stars were produced. . . . Concerning generation, and the nature of the soul, and many other subjects, they express views like those mentioned by the Greeks. They wrap up their doctrines about immortality and future judgement and kindred topics in allegories after the manner of Plato."[3] These brāhmaṇas were of a very independent spirit. Their best example is furnished by a sage of Taxila called Dandamis or Mandanis by the Greeks. When Alexander, who called himself the son of Zeus, sent an invitation to this sage to meet him, promising him great reward if he accepted his invitation and threatening him with death in case of refusal, Dandamis replied that he also was the son of Zeus as much as Alexander himself was, and asked the messenger to tell Alexander that Dandamis had no need of aught that was Alexander's and therefore would not go to him, but if Alexander wanted anything from Dandamis, he should himself go to Dandamis. The views that Dandamis expressed in his reply contain the substance of Upaniṣadic thought and are as follows:

> God, the supreme King, is never the author of insolent wrong, but is the Creator of light, of peace, of life, of water, of the body of man, and of souls and these he receives when death sets them free, being in no way subject to evil desire. He alone is the God of my homage, who abhors slaughter and instigates no wars. . . . Know this, however, that what Alexander offers me and the gifts he promises me, are all things to me utterly useless; but the things I prize, and of real use and worth, are these leaves which are my house, these blooming plants which supply me with dainty food, and the water which is my drink, while all other possessions and things which are amassed with anxious care, are wont to prove ruinous to those who amass them, and cause only sorrow and vexation, with which every poor mortal is fully fraught. But as for me, I lie upon the forest leaves, and having nothing which requires guarding, close my eyes in tranquil slumber, whereas had I gold to guard that would banish sleep. . . . Should Alexander cut off my head, he cannot also destory my soul. My head alone, now silent, will remain but the soul will go away to its Master, leaving the body like a torn garment upon the earth, whence also it was taken. I then, becoming spirit, shall ascend to my God.[4]

Dandamis provides a good example of the brāhmaṇas who were the custodians and disseminators of the Upaniṣadic thought in the Mauryan period. These brāhmaṇas were held in high esteem not only by the people of their country, but also by outsiders. Megasthenes has, as we have seen, said a lot about them, but his opinion about them is perhaps summed up in the following passage. "All that has been said regarding nature by the ancients is asserted also by philosophers out of Greece, on the one part in India by the Brachmane and on the other in Syria by the people called the Jews."[5]

The third branch of the Vedic religion which had a good number of followers in the Mauryan period may be called the theistic branch. In this branch stress was laid on *bhakti* or devotion to God as the most effective way to salvation. Pāṇini, the great Sanskrit grammarian, who lived and wrote at a time not later than the fifth century BCE refers to the devotees of Vāsudeva and his faithful friend Arjuna. Two inscriptions of the pre-Christian era found at Ghasundi and Nanaghat inform us that Saṅkarṣaṇa, the brother of Vāsudeva was also worshipped with him.[6]

Vāsudeva Kr̥ṣṇa, though engulfed in myths in later times, was doubtless a historical person who is mentioned in the ancient *Chāndogya Upaniṣad* as a son of Devakī and a disciple of the sage Ghora Āṅgirasa. He was both a great warrior and a great sage who laid emphasis on devotion to one God and on the performance of duty without caring for reward, and on the basis of whose teachings the celebrated ethical poem *Bhagavadgītā* was composed. By the time of the establishment of the Mauryan empire he had already been deified and probably made into an incarnation of Viṣṇu, the Protector of the universe. This is proved by a statement of Megasthenes. The Greek ambassador, while giving a fabulous account of the adventures of his country's hero Herakles in India, clearly identifies him with Kr̥ṣṇa in one of the passages which gives the valuable information that Kr̥ṣṇa had already been deified and begun to be worshipped in the region of India where he was believed to have been born. The passage is as follows.

"This Herakles is held in special honor by the Sourasenoi (Śūrasenas), an Indian tribe, who possess two large cities, Methora (Mathura) and Cleisobora (Krishnapura?) and through whose country flows a navigable river called Jobenes (Yamuna)."[7] The followers of Kṛṣṇa Vāsudeva were known as the *Bhāgvatas*. The simple and noble tenets of this sect attracted the Greeks also in due course of time as is evident from the inscription of Heliodorus engraved on a pillar at Besnagar in the state of Madhya Pradesh in India. On the other hand, it is possible that the worship of images of gods and deified persons in India, whose earliest mention is found in the fourth century BCE, received an impetus from the Greek practice of making images of gods. In any case, the Greek writers and the grammarian Patañjali both inform us that the image of Kṛṣṇa was already worshipped in the age of the Nandas, Mauryas, and Śuṅgas. We learn from Curtius that an image of Herakles (Kṛṣṇa) was carried in front of the army of Porus as he advanced against Alexander.[8] Similarly we learn from Patañjali that Keśava, i.e. Kṛṣṇa was one of the deified heroes whose images were worshipped in the temples in the Śuṅga period which immediately followed the Maurya period.

The second great religion of India in the time of Candragupta Maurya was Buddhism, founded by Gautama Buddha in the sixth century BCE, which put moral obligation in the front and taught that man was the maker of himself. It was probably followed by a considerable section of the population in most of northern India. Two great Buddhist councils held in the reigns of Ajātaśatru and Kālāśoka respectively had already made some contribution to the development of this religion. In the first council the *Dhamma Suttas* and the *Vinaya Suttas* of the Buddhist canon were for the first time recited. The second council was held at Vaiśālī in the reign of King Kālāśoka when practically the whole of the *Tripiṭaka*, the scripture of Buddhism is said to have been compiled. The three parts of the *Tripiṭaka*, which is in the Pāli language, were given the names *Suttapiṭaka*, *Vinayapiṭaka*, and *Abhidhammapiṭaka* respectively. The *Suttapiṭaka* is divided into five *Nikāya*s known as the *Dīgha Nikāya*, the *Majjhima Nikāya*, the *Saṁyutta Nikāya*, the *Aṅguttara Nikāya*, and the *Khuddaka Nikāya*. The last *Nikāya*, contains the celebrated *Dhammapada* and the *Jātaka* stories. The other two *Piṭaka*s are also divided into several parts. The last part of the *Abhidhammapiṭaka* known as the *Kathāvatthu* is believed to have been composed during the reign of Emperor Aśoka. The second council also had a debate on the conduct of the monks of Vaiśālī, which resulted in the division of the Buddhist church. The supporters of these monks came to be called the *Mahāsāṅghika*s, while those who disagreed with them were called the *Sthavira*s.

Megasthenes, as we have already seen, mentions two kinds of Indian philosophers known as the Brachmanes and the Sarmanes. There is no dispute regarding the identification of the Brachmanes with the Brāhmaṇas. The Sarmanes from their name appear to be Buddhist Śramaṇas or monks. Megasthenes' description of the Śramaṇas as reproduced by Strabo creates doubt whether they were really Buddhist monks, but that reproduced by Clemens of Alexandria, wherein Buddha himself is mentioned, removes all doubts. "Connected with the Sarmanai," we are told, "are the philosophers called the Hylobioi (forest dwellers) who neither live in cities nor even in houses. They clothe themselves with the bark of trees, and subsist upon acorns, and drink water by lifting it to their mouth with their hands. They neither marry nor beget children. They are those among the Indians who follow the precepts of Boutta, whom they honor as a god on account of his extraordinary sanctity."[9]

This description of forest dwelling Śramaṇas and the mention of the Buddha himself leaves no room for doubt that we have here one of the earliest accounts of the Buddhist order of monks, who are known from Buddhist sources to have shunned cities and villages.

Besides the brāhmaṇa philosophers and the Buddhist Śramaṇas, there were two other orders of ascetics known as the *Nirgrantha*s and the *Ājīvika*s respectively. The *Nirgrantha* order, better known as Jainism, was founded by Mahāvīra in the sixth century BCE. The name of the order, *Nirgrantha,* meant 'fetterless.' The *Nirgrantha*s were so-called because they were required to give up their worldly ties and even their clothes. They believed in the existence of soul in everything and desisted from killing or harming any form of life including the plants.

The order of *Nirgrantha*s of Jains was not only known to the Buddhist texts, but also appears to have been known to Megasthenes. The description given by Megasthenes of a particular order of philosophers is wholly applicable to the *Nirgrantha*s, though he has mistakenly called it a sect of brāhmaṇas. This is what Megasthenes says about the followers of this sect, "There is among the Brachmanes in India a sect of philosophers who adopt an independent life, and abstain from animal food and all victuals cooked by fire, being content to subsist upon fruits, which they do not so much as gather from the trees, but pick up when they have dropped to the ground. . . . . Throughout life they go about naked, saying that the body has been given by the Deity as a covering for the soul."[10]

The tradition recorded in the late Jain books gives a connected history of the Jain church. Bhadrabāhu was the head of the Jain church in the time of Candragupta Maurya and is said to have converted the emperor to the Jain faith. When a famine broke out in Magadha, Bhadrabāhu is said to have gone with his followers to Sravan Belgola in Karnataka. In his absence Sthūlabhadra was appointed head of the Jain church and he convoked a council of the *Nirgrantha* monks at Pāṭaliputra in which the Jain canon was fixed. Bhadrabāhu returned to Magadha after the famine had passed away and turned down the canon, fixed by the council of monks in his absence, as spurious. The Magadhan monks had also in the meantime begun to put on clothes, and this practice was also condemned by Bhadrabāhu as contrary to the teachings of Mahāvīra.[11] We do not know how far this traditional account is historical. The inscriptions of Sravan Belgola mention Bhadrabāhu and Candragupta, but they belong to the tenth century and therefore cannot be regarded as authentic. In any case since according to Hemacandra, Bhadrabāhu died in the sixteenth year of the reign of Candragupta, it is not possible to accept the tradition that Candragupta abdicated and went to Sravan Belgola with Bhadrabāhu.

The ascetic order of *Ājīvika*s was also, like Buddhism and Jainism, founded in the sixth century BCE. The name of the founder was Makkhali Gosāla. The word Makkhali corresponds to the Sanskrit Maskarin. It meant an ascetic who carried a bamboo staff (*maskara*) in his hand. The *ājīvika* ascetics were fatalists who thought that there was neither reward nor retribution for any action and that everything was dictated by fate. The *Ājīvika*s attained some importance in the Maurya period and were patronized by the Maurya emperors Aśoka and his grandson Daśaratha, but after the Maurya period this order began to decline and in due course became extinct.

We have enough material at our disposal to give a picture of Indian society in the Mauryan period. We learn from Kauṭilya that the Indian society was divided into four classes which had come to be called *varṇa*s. The main features of the present caste system, namely, the fact that no one can change his caste, had already come into existence in the Maurya period, but in other respects there was a lot of flexibility.

The four castes into which the Indian society of the Maurya period was divided were the brāhmaṇas, kṣatriyas, vaiśyas, and śūdras. Of these the first three were the castes into which the Āryan population of India was divided, while the śūdras were probably a heterogeneous group consisting of many tribes. The duties and functions of these four castes are thus given by Kauṭilya. "The duty of the brahman is study, teaching, performance of sacrifice, officiating at others' sacrificial performance and the giving and receiving of gifts. That of a kṣatriya is study, performance of sacrifice, giving gifts, military occupation and protection of life. That of a vaiśya is study, performance of sacrifice, giving gifts, agriculture, cattle breeding and trade. That of a śūdra is the serving of the twice born (the three upper castes), agriculture, cattle breeding, and trade, and the professions of artisans and court bards."[12] It appears that as a result of the influence of Buddhism the position of the śūdras in the society had improved, for they were allowed to follow the occupations of the vaiśyas. In time of need a brāhmaṇa could take up the military occupation, agriculture, cattle breeding or trade. A kṣatriya could similarly in time of need live by agriculture, cattle breeding or trade. The vaiśyas and śūdras were similarly permitted to take up the military occupation in time of need. As far as intermarriages between different castes and the status of the children born of such marriages is concerned, we learn from Kauṭilya that in the first three castes if a man of a higher caste married a woman of a lower caste, the offspring belonged to the father's caste.[13] Marriage between a man of a lower caste and a woman of a higher caste, even among the three upper castes, was not considered good by the authors of the *Dharmaśāstras* with whom Kauṭilya concurs, and hence the children born of such marriages have been stigmatized by these authors, but in actual practice even in such marriages the children were regarded as belonging to the caste of the father.[14] The offspring of marriage between a person of any of the three upper castes and a person of the śūdra caste was considered a *varṇa-saṅkara* (a person of mixed origin).

Megasthenes has divided the whole population of India into seven classes, perhaps on the analogy of Egypt. He is certainly wrong when, attributing to these classes the traits of what we call the caste system, he says that no one is allowed to marry out of his own caste or to exercise any calling or art except his own. This statement is not wholly true, as we have already seen, even with regard to the four actual castes. As far as these seven classes of Megasthenes are concerned, they are not castes, for the members of these classes were drawn from different castes. The classification is, however, not without value, for it throws light on the seven main occupations followed by the Indians of the Mauryan period. The following is the description of the seven classes by Megasthenes as quoted by Strabo.

The first class was formed by the collective body of philosophers, who, as we have already seen, included in their ranks the brāhmaṇa priests and the Buddhist Śramaṇas and probably also a very small number of Jain *munis*. About their general characteristics, which are clearly applicable to brāhmaṇa priests, we are told that "the philosophers are first in rank, but form the smallest class in point of number. Their services are employed privately by persons who wish to offer sacrifices or perform other sacred rites, and also publicly by the kings at what is called the Great Synod, wherein at the beginning of the new year all the philosophers are gathered together before the king at the gates, when any philosopher who may have committed any useful suggestion to writing, or observed any means for improving the crops and the cattle, or for promoting the public interests, declares it publicly. If any one is detected giving false information thrice, the law condemns him to be silent for the rest of his life, but he who gives sound advice is exempted from paying taxes or contributions."

The second class consisted of the husbandmen. Though the majority of them were probably vaiśyas, farmers of śūdra and even brāhmaṇa and kṣatriya castes were not unknown. These husbandmen according to Megasthenes were more numerous than the members of any other class. "They are," we are told, "in disposition most mild and gentle. They are exempted from military service and cultivate their lands undisturbed by any fear. They never go to town, either to take part in its tumults, or for any other purpose." We have already seen that in times of war too they were not disturbed by the soldiers of either side of the conflict. As far as the payment of revenue is concerned the Greek authors who have quoted Megasthenes widely differ. Diodorus says, "They pay a land tribute to the king, because all India is the property of the crown, and no private person is permitted to own land. Besides the land tribute they pay into the royal treasury a fourth part of the produce of the soil." Strabo, on the other hand, says this : "The whole of the land belongs to the Crown, and the husbandmen till it on condition of receiving as wages one-fourth of the produce." Lastly Arrian simply says : "They cultivate the soil and pay tribute to the kings and the independent cities (republics)." Arrian, as we can see is silent on state ownership of land, and he is doubtless closer to truth than the other two authors, for the idea of the whole state being the property of the king was unknown to Indian tradition and Kauṭilya too does not assert such ownership of the king. The other two Greek authors seem to have interpreted the statements of Megasthenes on the basis of their knowledge of the rules prevailing in other countries like Macedonia and Egypt.

The third class consisted of herdsmen and hunters by whom, no doubt, wild tribes like the Niṣādas are meant. "They alone," we are told, "are allowed to hunt, and to keep cattle, and to sell draught animals or let them out on hire. In return for clearing the land of wild beasts and fowls which devour the seeds sown in the fields, they receive an allowance of grain from the king. They lead a wandering life and live under tents."

The fourth class consisted of artisans. The majority of them were probably vaiśyas, but śūdra artisans must not have been rare. Many of them made implements which husbandmen and others found useful in their different callings. The armour-makers and shipbuilders, however, received wages and their victuals from the king for whom alone they worked. The general in command of the army supplied the soldiers with weapons, and the admiral of the fleet let out ships on hire for the transport both of passengers and merchandise.

The fifth class consisted of fighting men. Although the officers of this class probably mostly belonged to the kṣatriya caste, the rank and file must have been drawn from the castes of the vaiśyas and the śūdras. They gave themselves up to idleness and amusement in the times of peace, but were always ready, when occasion called, to take the field.

The sixth class consisted of overseers who must have been recruited from all castes. To them was assigned the duty of watching all that went on and making reports secretly to the king. Some were entrusted with the inspection of the city, and others with that in the army. They did not disdain from taking the help of the courtesans in the fulfilment of their duties.

The seventh class according to Megasthenes consisted of the counsellors and assessors of the king. In point of numbers this was a small class but it was distinguished by superior wisdom and justice, and from its ranks alone were chosen governors of provinces, deputy governors, superintendents of the treasury, generals of the army and the tribunals of justice.[15] Megasthenes has certainly erred in regarding all the high offices of state as belonging to one class. As a matter of fact the general of the army was usually a kṣatriya, but could also be and sometimes actually was a brāhmaṇa.[16] The ministers and judges were often but not invariably brāhmaṇas and many other high officers could be vaiśyas as well as brāhmaṇas and kṣatriyas. Thus while Cāṇakya, the Prime Minister of Candragupta was a brāhmaṇa, the governor of Surāṣṭra in his time was a vaiśya named Puṣyagupta.

For many centuries before the advent of the Mauryan period, the life of an Ārya had been divided in four *āśrama*s or stages, and the practice continued in the Mauryan period. The first stage was that of a *brahmacārin* or student when, after the *upanayana* ceremony, the boy went to study under a learned teacher and lived in strict discipline, observing celibacy and abjuring meat and drink. At about the age of twenty-four he married and became a *gṛhastha* or householder. After marrying away his children and becoming a grandfather, a man was expected to retire with his wife to some place outside the town and near the woods. In this stage he was called a *vānaprastha* or forest dweller and had again to lead a life of discipline. Many brāhmaṇas in this stage of life often started their own schools where students went to study. The last stage was that of a *parivrājaka* or *sannyāsin* who totally snapped all ties with the world, and, having become a wandering ascetic, travelled from place to place enlightening the people on various matters concerning religion and philosophy. Probably only a few brāhmaṇas opted for this stage.

Megasthenes has given a detailed description of the brāhmaṇa student and householder of the Mauryan period, pointing out the differences in their lifestyles. Although he has committed some mistakes which will be later pointed out, the description is very illuminating. This is what he says:

> The philosophers (i.e. Brahmans intending to study) have their abode in a grove in front of the city within a moderate-

> sized enclosure. They live in a simple style, and lie on beds of rushes or (deer) skins. They abstain from the animal food and sexual pleasures, and spend their time in listening to serious discourse. . . . After living in this manner for seven and thirty years, each individual retires to his own property, where he lives for the rest of his days in ease and security. They then array themselves in fine muslin, and wear a few trinkets of gold in their fingers and in their ears. They eat flesh but not that of animals employed in labor. They abstain from hot and highly seasoned food. They marry as many wives as they please with a view to have numerous children. For by having many wives greater advantages are enjoyed, and since they have no slaves, they have more need to have children around them to attend to their wants.[17]

This description though faithful on the whole suffers from some innocent mistakes. Thus his statement that every individual lived the life of a student for thirty-seven years is wrong, this being the extreme age limit up to which a person could in very exceptional cases protract his studies.[18] His statement that after finishing his studies every person lived for the rest of his days in ease is again mistaken, because there were undoubtedly at least some persons who after fulfilling all their duties towards their children became anchorites. Lastly he is not right in saying that the Brāhmaṇas married as many wives as they please because, having no slaves, they had more need to have children around to attend to their wants. In the first place, as far as this statment is concerned, it should be remembered that polygamy in ancient India was restricted to the members of the aristocratic class consisting of kings, princes, nobles and wealthy businessmen. The brāhmaṇas[19] and the common people were usually monogamous. The reason given by Megasthenes for the brāhmaṇas' need to have a large number of children is again wrong, for slavery, as we shall see later, did exist in the Maurya period, though it was so different from that prevalent in the west, that a Greek could not notice it.

Kauṭilya, like the authors of the ancient *Dharmasūtras*, mentions eight kinds of marriages,[20] but in reality there were only six. The first and the commonest, which is now the only form recognized in Hindu society, was the *Brāhma* marriage in which the parents of the girl marry her to a suitable young man after adorning her with ornaments. The second was the *Daiva* marriage in which the parents of the girl married her to an officiating priest at the time of a sacrifice. The third kind called *Ārṣa* must also have been prevalent in the Maurya period, because Megasthenes seems to refer to it when he says that Indians marry wives "giving in exchange a yoke of oxen."[21] The fourth kind that was approved for the Kṣatriyas was the *Gāndharva* which is the one prevalent in the west today. This type of marriage took place with the mutual consent of the boy and the girl without the intervention of the parents. The fifth and the sixth kinds of marriages, which were not considered good, were the *Rākṣasa* or marriage by capture of the girl and *Āsura* or marriage by purchase of the girl. The *Rākṣasa* marriage was, however, approved in the case of Kṣatriya if he captured or abducted a willing maiden,[22] or eloped with her, against the wish of her parents and kinsmen.[23]

The remarriage of widows was permitted even in the Vedic times and is also frankly recognized by Kauṭilya. The only condition for such a kind of marriage was that the widow forefeited whatever had been given to her by her father-in-law and her deceased husband; and if she happened to have sons also, she lost even her own property (*strīdhana*) which was given to her sons.[24]

What is most curious is that Kauṭilya also recognized a kind of divorce. The following passage from the *Arthaśāstra* makes it clear. "A woman hating her husband cannot dissolve her marriage with him against his will. Nor can a man dissolve his marriage with his wife against her will. But from mutual enmity divorce may be obtained." We are, however, told that divorce even on these grounds could be obtained only in the last three out of the six kinds of marriages. It is clear from these regulations that cases of divorce must have been rare and hence Megasthenes is silent on the subject.

The marriage rules mentioned above show that women in the Mauryan period occupied a fairly good position in the society. Although after the death of a man his property was divided among his sons, the widow was not only entitled to get food, clothing and shelter from her sons, but also had her own property called *strīdhana* which is defined by Kauṭilya as follows. "Means of subsistence as well as jewelry constitutes what is called the property of a woman. Means of subsistence valued at not less than two thousand *paṇas* shall be endowed in her name. There is no limit to jewelry. . . . On the death of her husband, a woman desirous to lead a pious life, shall at once receive not only her endowment and her jewelry, but also the balance of *śulka* due to her."[25]

According to Megasthenes all the Indians were free and not one of them was a slave.[26] But in the light of the *Arthaśāstra* we have to modify this statement. As a matter of fact slavery did exist, but a perusal of *Arthaśāstra* makes it clear that it was so different from the slavery which prevailed in the west, that a Greek could hardly notice it. It was forbidden to sell an Ārya or freeman (here including śūdra) into slavery except at his own option and dire necessity. "It is no crime," says Kauṭilya, "for Mlecchas[27] to sell or mortgage the life of their own offspring, but never shall an Ārya be subjected to slavery." He then proceeds to say that if a man is enslaved for inevitable reasons, he should be soon redeemed. "But if in order to tide over family troubles, to find money for fines or court decrees, or to recover the (confiscated) household implements, the life of an Ārya is mortgaged, they (his kinsmen) shall as soon as possible redeem him (from bondage); and more so if he is a youth or an adult capable of giving help." Moreover a slave in the west had no personal rights; his person was dead. In India, a *dāsa* was little worse than a servant as long as he was not redeemed; his offsprings being free even during his period of bondage. A *dāsa* could even earn independently if he got time from his master's work, and could regain his Āryahood if his independent income became equal to the value for which he was purchased. If a man abused or caused hurt to his slave, or employed the latter to do an ignoble work, the slave became free. Thus it is clear that although there were *dāsa*s in India, the kind of slavery prevalent in the west was non-existent in India.[28]

Arrian has given an interesting description of the dress worn by the Indians, which being made of cotton thread all the more attracted the Greeks, because cotton in its manufactured state was new to them. They have therefore described the Indians as clothed in garments made from wool which grew on trees. This is what Arrian says on the basis of the information given by Nearchus: "They (the Indians) wear an undergarment of cotton which reaches below the knee half way down to the ankles,[29] and also an upper garment which they throw partly over their shoulders and partly twist in folds round their head.[30] The Indians wear also earrings of ivory, but only such of them do this as are very wealthy, for all Indians do not wear them. Their beards, Nearchus tells us, they dye of one hue and another, according to taste . . . They wear shoes made of white leather, and these are elaborately trimmed while the soles are variegated, and made of great thickness, to make the wearer seem so much the taller."[31]

Strabo, on the testimony of Megasthenes, further tells us that "in contrast to the general simplicity of their style, they (the Indians) love finery and ornament. Their robes are worked in gold, and ornamented with precious stones, and they wear also flowered garments made of the finest muslin. Attendants walking behind hold up umbrellas over them, for they have high regard for beauty and avail themselves of every device to improve their looks."[32]

We are fortunate to possess sufficient details preserved from the writings of Megasthenes to understand what the Indian people were like. "The inhabitants," we are told, "having abundant means of subsistence, exceed in consequence the ordinary stature and are distinguished by their proud bearing."[33] They were simple in their manners and frugal. They disliked a great undisciplined multitude, and consequently they observed good order. They were noted for their high standard of morality, being generally truthful and honest. They seldom went to law and generally left their houses and property unguarded.[34] They did not rear monuments to the dead, but considered the virtues which men had displayed in life, and the songs in which their praises were celebrated, sufficient to preserve their memory after death.[35]

No nation, as no individual, however virtuous or progressive, can be expected to be perfect. Strabo, after recounting the virtues of the Indians, points out something which cannot be approved, in these words: "These things indicate that they possess good, sober sense; but there are other things they do which one cannot approve; for instance, that they eat always alone, and that they have no fixed hours when meals are to be taken by all in common, but each one eats when he feels inclined. The contrary custom would be better for the ends of social and civil life."[36] Some other weaknesses of the Indians of those times are known from the inscriptions of Aśoka and the *Arthaśāstra* of Kauṭilya. In the ninth pillar edict, Aśoka speaks with disapproval of the various *maṅgalas* or auspicious rites performed by the people and specially women in sickness, marriage, birth of a child and at the time of undertaking a journey. The *Arthaśāstra* bears testimony to the peoples' belief in witchcraft.[37] Kauṭilya also gives regulations about gambling which seems to have been a common vice among the aristocratic classes.[38] The same author gives elaborate regulations regarding liquor houses.[39] Megasthenes, however, perhaps keeping the brāhmaṇas in view, tells us that the people of India did not drink wine (the *soma* juice?) except at sacrifices.[40]

India in the Maurya period stood at a high level of economic prosperity. It had a large number of rich and prosperous cities. The information regarding the way in which the cities of those times were built has been preserved by Arrian. This is what he says: "Of their cities it is said that the number is so great that it cannot be stated with precision; but that such cities as are situated on the banks of rivers or on the seacoast are built of wood, for were they built of brick they would not last long — so destructive are the rains and also the rivers when they overflow their banks and inundate the plains; those cities, however, which stand on commanding situations and lofty eminences are built of brick and mud."[41]

Kauṭilya has preserved interesting details about the economic condition of the country. The system of traffic by barter had passed away, and coins were used for tran-sactions. In the pre-Maurya period punch-marked coins used to be issued by private persons. But if Kauṭilya mentions what was a fact, it is clear that the government of Candragupta issued and regulated coins. Kauṭilya speaks of a regular government mint.[42] The standard coin seems to have been the silver *paṇa*, which was probably of about 146 grains. There were also half, quarter and one-eighth of *paṇas*. The copper coin was called the *māṣaka*. A gold coin called the *suvarṇa* is also mentioned, but perhaps in its use was rare.

Of the industries of India agriculture has been the chief one since ancient times, and the Maurya period was no exception. Kauṭilya has given an account of the crops grown which included rice, barley, wheat, sesamum, linseed, mustard, pulses, sugarcane and cotton.[43] Megasthenes corroborates the account and gives further particulars, which are worth quoting. "In addition to cereals, there grows throughout India much millet, which is kept well watered by the profusion of river streams, and much pulse of different sorts, and rice also, and what is called *bosporum*, as well as many other plants useful for food, of which most grow spontaneously. The soil yields, moreover, not a few other edible products fit for the subsistence of animals, about which it would be tedious to write. It is accordingly affirmed that famine has never visited India, and that there has never been a general scarcity in the supply of nourishing food. For, since there is a double rainfall in the course of each year — one in the winter season, when the sowing of wheat takes place as in other countries, and the second at the time of the summer solstice, which is the proper season for sowing rice and *bosporum*, as well as sesamum and millet — the inhabitants of India almost always gather in two harvests annually; and even should one of the sowings prove more or less abortive they are always sure of the other crop. The fruits, moreover, of spontaneous growth, and the esculant roots which grow in marshy places and are of varied sweetness, afford abundant sustenance for man. The fact is, almost all the plains in the country have a moisture which is alike genial, whether it is derived from the rivers, or from the rains of the summer season which are wont to fall every year at a stated period with surprising regularity; while the great heat which prevails ripens the roots which grow in the marshes, and specially those of the tall reeds."[44]

It is clear from the above that there was no scarcity of crop in India at that time and that various factors tended to the prevention of famine. But in spite of all this, famine did sometimes occur. The traditions of the Jains record a great famine which occurred in the reign of Candragupta Maurya. The government, no doubt, adopted various relief measures when famine did occur. Kauṭilya has recorded several of them. The chief of them were the distribution of provision by government among the people, the employment of men to repair ruined buildings, request of help from the allies, exhorting the rich persons to contribute to the cause of famine relief and emigration of the population to regions having abundant harvest.[45]

The textile industry seems to have been the one most widespread after agriculture. Megasthenes as we have already seen has highly praised the robes worn by Indians for their fineness. Kauṭilya gives elaborate regulations about weaving, which prove the importance of this industry. It is noteworthy that it was a home industry, and women did much of the spinning.[46] Cotton fabrics of Banaras, Bengal, Kaliṅga and Madurā were considered to be the best, according to the *Arthaśāstra*. The same work also mentions the manufacture of silk, hemp and woollen materials. It is surprising to note that the blankets of Nepal were famous even at that period.[47]

The mining industry was also sufficiently advanced. Precious stones as well as metals formed the objects of mining. The metals known were gold (*suvarṇa*), silver (*rupyā*), iron (*kālāyasa*), copper (*tāmra*), bronze (*kāṁsya*), lead (*sīsa*), tin (*trapu*) and brass (*ārakūṭa*).[48] Megasthenes has also recorded his observations on the subject. "And while the soil bears on its surface all kinds of fruits which are known to cultivation, it has also underground numerous veins of all sorts of metals, for it contains much gold and silver, and copper and iron in no small quantity, and even tin and other metals, which are employed in making articles of use and ornament, as well as implements and accoutrements of war."[49] Indeed India was so rich in gold that fables became current that there were gold-digging ants in India.[50] There was no paucity of precious stones also, and Kauṭilya has carefully noted the different colours and qualities of diamonds (*vajra*), rubies (*padmarāga*), beryls (*vaidūrya*), sapphires (*indranīla*), and crystals (*sphaṭika*).[51]

The art of smelting metals was well-known and Kauṭilya specifies the characteristics of various metallic ores.[52] We have seen from the account given by Megasthenes that whereas the blacksmiths and other metal workers made implements for husbandmen, armours and weapons for soldiers, and articles of daily use for civilians, the goldsmiths made gold and silver ornaments of various kinds. There were also skilled carpenters who made not only small articles of use and decoration, but also ships, carts, chariots, and the wood work of houses. An indisputable testimony to the perfection of this craft in the Mauryan period is furnished by the wooden platforms that have been dug up in the vicinity of Patna.[53]

One of the most ancient arts in which Indian craftsmen have excelled is ivory work. The *Jātaka*s have several references to ivory workers. The description of the wealthy men of the Mauryan period by Arrian as wearing ivory earrings shows that it was a flourishing art in that period.

Another well-known industry of the Mauryan period was that of the leather worker. Kauṭilya mentions a wide variety of skins distinguished by their place of origin as well as colour and size.[54] Arrian's description of the beautiful white shoes worn by wealthy Indians proves the skill of the leather worker of those times.

Trade was in a flourishing condition in the Maurya period. Different places in the country had already gained special reputation for certain things. We have already seen that cotton fabrics of some places were looked upon as specially fine.

Southern India was similarly famous for conch-shells, diamonds, pearls and gold according to Kauṭilya.[55] Indian trade, however, was not limited within the country. Even before the Maurya time, India had maintained trade relations with Babylon and other countries.[56] These relations became all the more brisk in the Maurya period, as is proved by the creation of a special board for foreigners. The wise policy of friendship with Hellenistic powers pursued by Candragupta must have led to the expansion of Indian trade with West Asia and Egypt. The charming Indian peacocks, ivory, pearls, pigments and dyes and many other things were exported from India. Among articles of import Kauṭilya praises China silk, which proves that there was some traffic even with China.[57] This trade was carried on partly by the land route and partly by the sea route. Even an early Buddhist work, the *Bāveru Jātaka*, refers to a trading journey to Babylon by sea. Kauṭilya also mentions sea voyage and recommends that the route along and close to the shore is better, as it touches many trading port towns.[58]

A special feature of the economic life of that period was corporate activity. People following the same profession even though not belonging to the same caste, formed their own *śreṇī*, which was much like the medieval guild of Europe. The *śreṇī*s were recognized by the government and had many rights, such as deciding cases of dispute among members of the same *śreṇī*. The head of the *śreṇī* was called the *Śreṣṭhin*.[59] Another institution representing corporate life was the system of *sambhūya samutthāna*, which was much like the joint stock companies of the present-day. This kind of business corporation was established by several persons contributing some share, and when the profits were earned they were divided among the members in proportion to the share of each member.[60]

Much of the prosperity of trade depends upon roads. The Maurya government, as we have already seen, gave top priority to the building and maintenance of roads. The different provinces of the empire were connected with each other by a network of roads. A royal road ran from Puṣkalāvatī in the north-west frontier of the empire via Taxila and other cities to Pāṭaliputra and thence to the mouths of the Gaṅgā, and was the forerunner of the modern Grand Trunk Road. The vehicles used for journeying on the road are thus mentioned by Arrian. "The animals used by the common sort for riding on are camels and horses and asses while the wealthy use elephants — for it is the elephant which in India carries royalty. The conveyance which ranks next in honour is the chariot and four; the camel ranks third; while to be drawn by a single horse is considered no distinction at all."[61]

Notes

1. McCrindle, *Ancient India : Megasthenes and Arrian*, Fragm. I (40).
2. Ibid., Fragm. XXVII.
3. Ibid., Fragm. XLI.
4. Ibid., Fragm. LV.
5. Ibid., Fragm. XLII.
6. The worship of Kṛṣṇa, with his faithful ally Arjuna and his brother Saṅkarṣaṇa may be compared to the worship of Rāma in later times with his faithful ally Hanuman and his brother Lakṣmaṇa.
7. McCrindle, *Ancient India: Megasthenes and Arrian, Indika of Arrian*, VIII.
8. McCrindle, *Invasion of India by Alexander the Great*, p. 208.
9. McCrindle, *Ancient India : Megasthenes and Arrian*, Fragm. XLIII.
10. Ibid., Fragm. LIV.
11. This was the beginning of the division of the Jain community into two sects known as the Digambara and the Śvetāmbara.
12. *Arthaśāstra*, I, 3 (Shamasastry's translation).
13. The only exception is the offspring of a marriage between a man of the brāhmaṇa caste and a woman of the vaiśya caste who is called an *Ambaṣṭha*, but in actual practice the *Ambaṣṭha* must have been regarded a brāhmaṇa.

14. According to Buddhist sources, the mother of Emperor Aśoka was a brāhmaṇa lady but Aśoka, like Yadu and Turvaśa of the Vedic age, was considered a kṣatriya.
15. McCrindle, *Ancient India : Megasthenes and Arrian*, Fragm. XXXIII. *Indika of Arrian* XI & XII.
16. The general of the time of Bṛhadratha, the last Maurya emperor, was a brāhmaṇa, named Puṣyamitra Śuṅga.
17. McCrindle, *Ancient India : Megasthenes and Arrian*, Fragm. XLI.
18. *Manusmṛti*, III, 1.
19. The great *ṛṣis* of the Vedic age were as a general rule monogamous, for in most of the cases that we know a *ṛṣi* had only one wife. Thus the name of the wife of the ancient *ṛṣi* Cyavana was Sukanyā. The name of the wife of his descendant Ṛcīka was Satyavatī. The wife of Ṛcīka's son Jamadagni was Reṇukā. The name of Vasiṣṭha's wife was Arundhatī. The wife of Agastya was Lopāmudrā. Yājñavalkya alone among the great *ṛṣis* of ancient times had two wives named Maitreyī and Kātyāyanī.
20. *Arthaśāstra*, III, 2.
21. McCrindle, *Ancient India : Megasthenes and Arrian*, Fragm. XXVII.
22. The abduction of Rukmiṇī by Kṛṣṇa, of Subhadrā by Arjuna, of Vāsavadattā by Udayana, and of Saṁyogitā by Pṛthvīrāj are some of the examples of this kind of marriage.
23. Of the remaining two types, the *prājāpatya* is only a variety of the *Brāhma*, while the *paiśāca* is a degraded form of marriage by capture. The *Āpastamba Dharmasūtra* (II, 5, 11-12) actually mentions only six kinds of marriages, omitting the *prājāpatya* and the *paiśāca*.
24. *Arthaśāstra*, III, 2.
25. Ibid.
26. McCrindle, *Ancient India : Megasthenes and Arrian*, Fragm. XXVI.
27. The word *mleccha* was used for foreigners by the ancient Indians in the same sense and fashion as the word barbarian was used by the ancient Greeks.
28. *Arthaśāstra*, III, 13.
29. This undergarment was no doubt what is now called the *dhotī*.
30. Nearchus has by mistake turned two garments, the *dupaṭṭā* and the *uṣṇīṣa* (turban) into one.
31. McCrindle, *Ancient India : Indika of Arrian*, Fragm. XVI.

32. McCrindle, *Ancient India : Megasthenes and Arrian*, Fragm. XXVII.
33. Ibid., Fragm. I.
34. Ibid., Fragm. XXVII.
35. Ibid., Fragm. XXVI.
36. Ibid., Fragm. XXVII.
37. *Arthaśāstra*, XIV.
38. Ibid., III, 20.
39. Ibid., II, 25.
40. McCrindle, *Ancient India : Megasthenes and Arrian*, Fragm. XXVII.
41. McCrindle, *Ancient India : Indika of Arrian*, Fragm. X.
42. *Arthaśāstra*, II, 12.
43. Ibid., II.
44. McCrindle, *Ancient India : Megasthenes and Arrian*, Fragm. I.
45. *Arthaśāstra*, IV, 3.
46. Ibid., II, 23.
47. Ibid., II, 11.
48. Ibid., II, 17.
49. McCrindle, *Ancient India : Megasthenes and Arrian*, Fragm. I.
50. Ibid., Fragm. XXXIX.
51. *Arthaśāstra*, II, 11.
52. Ibid., II, 12.
53. *Archaeological Survey of India*, 1912-13, 53ff.
54. *Arthaśāstra*, II, 11.
55. Ibid., III, 12.
56. For a detailed study of this subject the reader is referred to Dr. Radha Kumud Mookerji's excellent book *History of Indian Shipping*.
57. *Arthaśāstra*, II, 11.
58. Ibid., VII, 12.
59. For this *vide* Mazumdar, *Corporate Life in Ancient India*.
60. *Arthaśāstra*, II, 14.
61. McCrindle, *Ancient India : Indika of Arrian*, Fragm. XVII.

6

Literature and Art

A PROSPEROUS reign always has a stimulating effect on the activities of the human mind. Unfortunately very little is known about the intellectual achievements of the people in the reign of Candragupta, but the little that is known is sufficient to give an idea of the literary and artistic deve-lopment of the age.

Indian literature was already considerable, and the art of writing had made it greatly accessible. The Vedic literature consisting of the Vedas, the *Brāhmaṇa*s and about a dozen genuine *Upaniṣad*s was already ancient. Even the six *Vedāṅga*s — *śikṣā* (phonetics), *kalpa* (ritual), *vyākaraṇa* (grammar), *nirukta* (etymology), *chanda*s (metrics), and *jyotiṣa* (astronomy) are mentioned by Kauṭilya;[1] and Yāska, Pāṇini and also perhaps Piṅgala had already composed their famous works on etymology, grammar, and metrics respectively. The oldest *Kalpa* manuals consisting of *Dharmasūtra*s, *Śrautasūtra*s and *Gṛhyasūtra*s had also, no doubt, come into existence.

Coming to the epic and Purāṇic literature, we find that the original *Rāmāyaṇa* of Vālmīki and the kernel of the *Mahābhārata* must have already existed, for Kauṭilya refers to some of their characters and events.[2] Some of the oldest Purāṇas in their original form had definitely come into existence long before the advent of the Mauryan period as is proved by the testimony of both Kauṭilya and Megasthenes. While Kauṭilya merely mentions the Purāṇa as a class of literature,[3] Megasthenes even shows his acquaintance with the main contents of the Purāṇas, for, identifying the first Āryan king, Manu, of the Purāṇas with the Greek god Dionysos, he has made the statement that from Dionysos (Manu) to Sandrakottos (Candragupta) the Indians counted 153 kings.[4] The actual number of kings from Manu to Candragupta in the present Purāṇas is 135, and the number mentioned by Megasthenes is so close to it that, no doubt, it reminds about the antiquity of the Purāṇas and their genealogies.

Of the six orthodox philosophical systems Kauṭilya mentions the Sāṅkhya and Yoga.[5] The other four systems, namely, the Mīmāṁsā and Vedānta, and the Nyāya and Vaiśeṣika, whose authoritative works have been composed in the ancient *sūtra* style also must have been in existence in that period. It is surprising that the atheistic Lokāyata or Cārvāka system, noted for its rational approach had already come into existence since it is mentioned by Kauṭilya.[6]

Among the sciences known in that period we have already mentioned astronomy which was regarded as one of the six *Vedāṅgas*. The science of medicine had also sufficiently advanced in this period. Arrian assures us that Indian doctors could cure even snakebite, although the Greek physicians were unable to do so.[7]

At the beginning of the Mauryan period the Āryan speech had spread practically in the whole of northern India which was given the name of Āryāvarta. This speech had, like the other languages of the world, two forms, the language of the elite and the language of the common people, which in course of time came to be called Sanskrit and Prākṛt respectively. The Sanskrit language had changed much from its earliest stage as found in the *Ṛgveda*. It was, however, still a living language, and is called *Bhāṣā* or the spoken language by Pāṇini. The

Prākṛt or speech of the common people had in the Mauryan period three main varieties as revealed in the inscriptions of Aśoka. One of them, spoken in the home province of the empire consisting of the eastern U.P. and Bihar then known as Kosala, Kāśī, Videha, Aṅga and Magadha, may be called the Prācya or Eastern Prākṛt. The second variety was that spoken in the Madhyadeśa or Midland comprising Haryana, Delhi, western U.P. and eastern Rajasthan then known as Kuru, Pañcāla, Śūrasena and Matsya. The third variety was the one spoken in the North-west Frontier Province and the land of the five rivers then known as Gandhāra, Kekaya and Madra. The literary form of the Midland Prākṛt came to be called Pāli and became the language of the Buddhist scriptures. The script in which these languages were written was known as Brāhmī.

The literature of the Maurya period was composed either in Sanskrit or in Eastern Prākṛt or in Pāli and may therefore be classified under these three heads. Owing to the well-known deficiency of dates in ancient Indian history, we can definitely assign to this period only a few works, which probably constitute only a fragment of the total literary output of that period. But the works which are known to belong to this period are important enough to constitute a literature in themselves.

The most important author of the age was Viṣṇugupta Cāṇakya, also known as Kauṭilya by his *gotra* or family name. Since the Kauṭilya family belonged to the Vatsa or Vātsyāyana group of the Bhṛgu clan of brāhmaṇas, Cāṇakya has also been called Vātsyāyana by one Sanskrit author who regards him as a Drāmila or southerner.[8] Born of poor brāhmaṇa parents, he received his education at Taxila according to tradition.[9] He then by his shrewdness and ability, became the chief counsellor of Candragupta and, according to some authorities, continued to guide the affairs of the successor of his master after the latter's death.[10] He is famous both as an author and a statesman. There can be no doubt that he was a great man of his age.

The most famous work attributed to this great man under his family name Kauṭilya is the *Arthaśāstra*. This work, as its name indicates, is a book on political economy and the art of government. It is mainly a prose work, divided into fifteen *adhikaraṇa*s or books, each subdivided into numerous chapters. It deals with the duties of kings, administration of public affairs, law and judiciary, relation with foreign powers, methods of warfare, and secret means to injure an enemy. The book has been condemned by many critics, including such early authors as Bāṇa,[11] on the score of many undesirable things advocated in it, such as the practice of witchcraft and the institution of espionage. No doubt there is much to be said against these and similar other things occurring in the *Arthaśāstra*. But in judging a book we have to look at both the good and bad sides as well as the circumstances in which it was composed. The condition of India was very unsettled at the time of the rise of the Maurya empire, and all kinds of means might have been considered necessary to restore peace with honour. But the same author has advocated things which deserve nothing but praise. The observation of an eminent scholar may be quoted to show the attitude of Kauṭilya towards slavery, and the position of the śūdra. "In regard to slavery, Kauṭilya's attitude stands apart as a glowing light of liberalism and humanity in a barbaric age. While his contemporary Aristotle was justifying slavery as a divine and a beneficent human institution not only sanctioned by nature, but also justified by the circumstances of social existence, he denounced it and strove to abolish it — characterizing it as a custom which could exist only among the savage Mlecchas. He boldly enunciated that among Āryas (freeborn) none should be unfree or enslaved. His definition of the Ārya was not narrow. According to him, the śūdra was equally an Ārya with members of the higher castes."[12] Cāṇakya was one of the pioneers to include the śūdra within the Āryan fold, and his motive must have been to strengthen Āryāvarta.

His views on other social matters are also generally liberal and commendable. He was, moreover, not without his admirers, for Kāmandaka, the author of *Nītisāra*, has praised him highly.[13] We may therefore conclude, in the words which Sir Frederic Pollock wrote about another statesman,[14] that of all the opinions about Cāṇakya's object in this book, ranging from the vulgar prejudice that he was a cynical counsellor of iniquity to the panegyric of those who regard him as one of the great preparers and champions of Indian unity, the latter at all events contains more truth than the former.

Cāṇakya is also the reputed author of a collection of witty aphorisms. To him are also ascribed a large number of verses on *nīti* or wise conduct.[15] He is even credited with writing on medicine, and in this capacity is known to Arabic writers as Sanaq.[16] No work of his on the subject, however, is known to have survived.

There can be no doubt that many Sanskrit writers must have produced works of merit in this period of affluence and prosperity but our ignorance of the chronology of most of the ancient Sanskrit works prevents us from assigning any of them definitely to the Mauryan period. Yet there are two famous works which appear to belong to the Mauryan period. One of these is the *Kāmasūtra* of Vātsyāyana, which because of its resemblance with the *Arthaśāstra* in language and style can with great probability be assigned to the Mauryan period. The other work is the celebrated *Nāṭyaśāstra* of Bharata which too can hardly have been written at a time later than the Mauryan period.

The greatest Prākṛt author of the age was Bhadrabāhu, the Jain pontiff. According to *Sthavirāvalī*, Bhadrabāhu was the sixth Sthavira after Mahāvīra. He was the disciple of Yaśobhadra. He lived and wrote during the reign of Candragupta. During the great famine that occurred in the time of Candragupta, Bhadrabāhu repaired to the south and there died by *samādhi*.

According to some accounts he was accompanied by Candragupta. But this does not seem to be correct, as according to Hemacandra, Bhadrabāhu died in the sixteenth year of Candragupta's reign. Bhadrabāhu is the reputed author of many Jain Prākṛt works. The most famous of these is the *Kalpasūtra*. The book is divided into three parts, namely *Jina caritra* (lives of *Jinas*), *Sthavirāvalī* (list of *Sthaviras*) and *Samācarī* (rules for *Yatis*). It is doubtful if the whole of this book is the work of Bhadrabāhu. Jacobi thinks that the list of *Sthaviras* contained in this book was probably added by Devardhi, the editor of the *Siddhānta*. Professor Weber ascertained that the whole *Kalpasūtra* is incorporated as the eighth lecture in the *Dasasūtra Skandha*, which is included in the ten *Niryuktis* attributed to Bhadrabāhu.

The only important Pāli work of the Maurya period was the Buddhist *Kathāvatthu*, ascribed to Maudgaliputra Tiṣya. It was, however, composed in the reign of Aśoka and does not strictly belong to the period we are dealing with.

All the learning contained in this vast literature of Mauryan and pre-Mauryan times was disseminated at the different centres of education. The most famous of such centres was Taxila. Many foreigners as well as Indian princes and sons of brāhmaṇas and common people flocked to it as to a university town. Another famous seat of learning was Vārāṇasī or Banaras, which has maintained its ancient glory undiminished to the present-day. The third important centre of education was Ujjain in western India. Pāṭaliputra, the capital of the Maurya empire, besides being politically and commercially the most important city of India was also a centre of education.

It is obvious from this brief survey that the reign of Candragupta was not devoid of literary achievements and educational facilities. In the field of arts also the success attained in that remote period by Indians was by no means insignificant, as is clear from the following observation of Megasthenes: "They are also found to be well skilled in the arts as might be expected of men who inhale a pure air and drink the finest water."[17] We shall briefly note the development of the chief arts in the Mauryan period.

Among fine arts music, dance and drama take precedence over others. The art of music in India goes back to Vedic times, and one of the four Vedas, the *Sāmaveda*, is a collection of prayers meant to be sung. In the Mauryan period it was already a highly developed art. Kauṭilya seversal times refers to singers (*gāyaka*s) and players on musical instruments (*vādaka*s),[18] and specifically lays down that the musical instruments (*ātodya*) with which the musicians entertained the king were not to be taken out of the palace.[19] Some of the instruments in vogue at that time were the *vīṇā* (lute), the *veṇu* (flute) and the *mr̥daṅga* (drum).[20] Kauṭilya's repeated reference to *nartaka*s[21] proves the prevalence of the art of dancing. The histrionic art too originated quite early in India. Pāṇini already refers to the *Naṭasūtra*s of Śilālin and Kr̥śaśva.[22] The development of this art in the Mauryan period is proved by the testimony of both Kauṭilya and Patañjali. Kauṭilya not only refers to *naṭa*s or actors[23] but even to *prekṣā*s or dramatic shows.[24] Patañjali, who lived towards the end of the Mauryan period, clearly mentions the staging of the plays *Kaṁsavadha* and *Balibandha* and even refers to the actor who feels the *rasa* which he enacts.[25] The combined testimony of Kauṭilya and Patañjali thus proves that the histrionic art was in a developed stage in the reign of Candragupta Maurya.

Painting has always held a high place among fine arts. We learn from Buddhist writings that fresco painting was already well-known. The following passage of Prof. Rhys Davids about painters in Buddhist India may be quoted in this connection. "They were mostly house painters. The wood work of the houses was often covered with fine *chunam* plaster and decorated with painting. But they also painted frescoes. These passages tell us of pleasure houses, adorned with painted figures and patterns, belonging to the kings of Magadha and Kosala, and such frescoes were no doubt similar in character to, but of course in an earlier style than, the well-known ancient frescoes of the seventh and eighth centuries CE on the Ajanta caves and of the fifth century on the Sigri Rock in Ceylon."[26] The fact that Kauṭilya several times refers to the art of painting[27] shows that it not only continued but must have made rapid strides in the Mauryan period under the patronage of an enlightened government.

The art of sculpture reached its high water mark in the Mauryan period under the patronage of Emperor Aśoka. The cutting and polishing of stones was, in the words of Dr. Vincent Smith, "carried to such perfection that it is said to be a lost art beyond modern powers."[28] That this art was already in a developed stage in the time of Candragupta Maurya is proved by the testimony of Megasthenes who while describing the palace of the Maurya monarch refers to its gilded pillars adorned with golden vines and silver birds and furnished with richly carved tables and chairs of state." Unfortunately, among the ancient pieces of sculpture that have been discovered in recent times, there is none which can be definitely assigned to the time of Candragupta. Two statues of *yakṣa*s discovered near Patna and now in the Indian Museum, Calcutta, one statue of a *yakṣa* found at Parkham and now in the Mathura Museum, one statue of a Yakṣiṇī discovered at Didarganj and another colossal *yakṣiṇī* statue found at Besnagar were assigned to early Maurya period by specialists because of their polish, but this view is now contested.[29] It is possible that the uninscribed Basarh-Bakhira pillar, which is artistically inferior to the inscribed pillars of Aśoka, was constructed in the reign of Candragupta.

Architecture has been considered the queen of arts and a survey of it is indispensable in a review of the progress of art in the Maurya period. This art had already made much progress in the pre-Maurya period, and we hear in the Jātakas of seven storyed palaces (*sattabhūmaka pāsāda*) of rich men. In the Maurya period this art was in a highly developed stage, as is proved by the description of Pāṭaliputra by Megasthenes. This great city with its 570 towers and 64 gates must have contained many stately buildings and charming gardens with blooming flowers as indicated by its other name Kusumapura, the city of flowers. The most magnificent building in this city was the palace of Emperor Candragupta which according to Megasthenes surpassed in splendour the palaces of Susa and Ekbatana.[30] The excavations at the site of the village Kumrahar carried on by Dr. Spooner have disclosed the remains of a mighty pillared hall of Mauryan date. This in all probability formed part of the palace of Candragupta himself.

The stone fragments of the pillars of this hall were found among ashes buried beneath old brick walls probably belonging to the Gupta period. Beneath the ashes was a layer of 9 feet of silt which covered the original floor of the hall. According to Dr. Spooner the silt was deposited on the floor of the hall by a flood which occurred somewhere about the time of Christ, and then, after some centuries, the portion above the silt was burnt down by a fire, which accounts for the ashes lying mixed with stone fragments above the silt. In connection with the woodwork of the superstructure Dr. Spooner has made the following remarks. "Judging from the timbers that have been preserved to us, it is clear that the woodwork of the superstructure and the room must have been extremely solid and massive, and that the heat of the final conflagration must have been enormous. It is evident that it sufficed to crack off innumerable fragments from that portion of the columns which rose above the silt, and also to expand the metal bolts which fitted into the socket holes observable in the top fragments of pillars which we have recovered."[31]

According to Dr. Spooner this Maurya hall was built on the model of the pillared hall at Persepolis. Dr. Smith, however, observed that the resemblance of the Maurya buildings with the Persian palace at Persepolis was not definitely established.

Interaction between Persia, Greece and India

The three great branches of the Āryan people, the Persians, the Greeks and the Indians, carved out three great empires, one after the other, between the sixth century BCE and the fourth century BCE. The first of these was the Persian empire of Darius I. The second was the Greek empire of Alexander. The third was the Indian empire of Candragupta. The rise of these empires brought the three nations into close contact with each other, as a result of which there was a good deal of give and take that continued for centuries. The Achaemenian empire of Darius being the earliest of the three empires, the Greeks as well as the Indians were influenced by its political institutions. The usage of appointing subordinate rulers in the provinces of an empire was borrowed both by the Greeks and the Indians from Persia. The designation of such a ruler which is *satrapes* in Greek and *kṣatrapa* in Sanskrit owes its origin to an old Persian word *khsatra-pava*. The Persians also in course of time borrowed from India whatever attracted them. The game of chess, for example, which is called *caturaṅga* in Sanskrit travelled to Persia and became *shatranj* in the Persian language.

Contacts between India and Greece had certainly begun in as early as the sixth century BCE. The University of Taxila was a centre of learning of international repute where Indian and foreign students came into close contact. It is possible that foreign languages like Persian and Greek were taught there as optional subjects. Pāṇini, the great Sanskrit grammarian is believed to have been a student of this university, and he was familiar with the Greek script which he mentions as Yavanānī (script of the Yavanas or Ionians).[32] Through this contact Indian philosophy and mathematics travelled to the West and influenced the Greek intellectuals. Thus the doctrine of Empedocles that nothing can arise which has not existed before, and that nothing can be annihilated is clearly based on the Sāṅkhya doctrine of the eternity of matter. Another Greek philosopher Pythagoras shows very clear influence of Indian philosophy and science on his doctrines. "Almost all the doctrines ascribed to him," to quote Prof. Macdonell,[33] "religious, philosophical, mathematical, were known in India in the sixth century BCE. The coincidences are so numerous that their cumulative force becomes considerable. The transmigration theory, the assumption of five elements, the Pythagorean theorem in geometry, the prohibition as to eating beans, the religio-philosophical character of the Pythagorean fraternity and the mystical speculations of the Pythagorean school, all have their parallels in ancient India. The doctrine of metempsychosis in the case of Pythagoras appears without any connection or explanatory background and was regarded by the Greeks as of foreign origin. He could not have derived it from Egypt, as it was not known to the ancient Egyptians. In spite, however, of later tradition, it seems impossible that Pythagoras should have made his way to India, at so early a date, but he could quite well have met Indians in Persia."

Some of the Indian religions also attracted the Greeks. The Bhāgavata sect of the Vedic religion with its noble and simple teachings was the earliest to draw persons of Greek origin into its fold as is evident from the inscription of Heliodorus. The other great religion of India to which many foreigners including the Greeks were converted was Buddhism. The most notable Greek convert to this religion was King Menander who ruled in the north-west of India in the second century BCE and who is well-known in the Buddhist writings under the name of Milinda.

Indians in their turn learned several things from the Greeks. In the numismatic art the Greeks excelled the Indians, and the fine silver coins of the Indian king Saubhūti betray very clear Greek influence. Another thing in which the Indians were influenced by the Greeks was the art of sculpture, and the Gāndhāra sculpture bears witness to this influence. The third thing for whose knowledge the Indians were indebted to Greece in some measure was the science of the heavenly bodies, particularly astrology in which the proficiency of the Greeks has been expressly acknowledged by the Indians.[34]

Notes

1. *Arthaśāstra*, I, 3.
2. Ibid., I, 6.
3. Ibid., I, 5.
4. McCrindle, *Ancient India : Indika of Arrian*, Fragm. IX.
5. *Arthaśāstra*, I, 2.
6. Ibid.
7. McCrindle, *Ancient India : Indika of Arrian*, Fragm. XV.
8. *vātsyāyano mallanāgaḥ kauṭilyaś caṇakātmajaḥ. drāmilaḥ pakṣilasvāmī viṣṇugupto 'ṅgulaś ca saḥ. — Abhidhāna Cintāmaṇi.*
9. Vide *Mahāvaṁsa ṭīkā* and *Pariśiṣṭaparvan*.
10. Tārānātha and Hemacandra have both preserved this tradition.
11. *kiṁ vā teṣāṁ sāmprataṁ yeṣām atinṛśaṁsaprāyopade-śanirghṛṇa-kauṭilyaśāstraṁ pramāṇam*, etc. — *Kādambarī*.
12. N.C. Bandopadhyaya, *Kauṭilya*, p. 211.
13. *Nīti śāstrāmṛtaṁ dhīmān arthaśāstramahodadheḥ Samuddadhre namastasmai Viṣṇuguptāya vedhase.* — *Nītisāra* of Kāmandaka.
14. Machaevelli, with whom Cāṇakya is often, though rather inappositely, compared.

15. These verses have been collected and edited by Dr. Ludwik Sternbach and published in four volumes under the title of *Cāṇakya Niti Text Tradition* by the Vishveshvaranand Vedic Research Institute, Hoshiarpur, Punjab, India.
16. Keith, *History of Sanskrit Literature*, p. 505.
17. McCrindle, *Ancient India: Megasthenes and Arrian*, Fragm. I, 36.
18. *Arthaśāstra*, II, 1, 27.
19. Ibid., I, 21.
20. Ibid., II, 1, 27.
21. Ibid.
22. *Aṣṭādhyāyī*, IV, 3, 10-11.
23. *Arthaśāstra*, II, 1, 27.
24. Ibid., XIII, 2.
25. *Mahābhāṣya*, V, 2, 59.
26. Rhys Davids, *Buddhist India*, p. 96.
27. *Arthaśāstra* I, 16; II, 27.
28. *Oxford History of India*, Pt. I, 2nd edn., p. 113.
29. Nihar Ranjan Ray in *Age of the Nandas and Mauryas*, pp. 378-84.
30. Nihar Ranjan Ray (*Age of the Nandas and Mauryas*, p. 357) seems to think that the palace of Pāṭaliputra reminded Megasthenes of the palaces of Susa and Ekbatana because of its similarity with them. Megasthenes, however, only says that the Mauryan palace surpassed in splendour the palaces of Susa and Ekbatana. A palace need not be similar to another palace in order to surpass it.
31. *Archaeological Survey of India*, 1912-13, p. 63.
32. *Aṣṭādhyāyī*, IV, 1, 49.
33. *A History of Sanskrit Literature*, chapter 16.
34. A stanza occurring in the *Gārgī Saṁhitā* may be quoted for the curious reader's benefit:

    yavanā hi mlecchās teṣu samyak śastram idaṁ sthitam
    Rṣivat tāpi pūjayante kiṁ punar devavad dvijāḥ.

    "The Greeks are barbarians, yet the science of astrology is well established among them. They too are therefore honoured like seers. How much more so than the god-like Brāhmaṇas."

7

Achievements of Candragupta

A REVIEW of the life and career of Candragupta can hardly be complete without a survey of the importance of his achievements. It is strange that a personage who, in ancient times, captured the imagination of Hindu, Buddhist, Jain, Greek and Roman authors alike, has been comparatively ignored in modern times. We shall here discuss his place in history on the ground of his achievements.

Candragupta began his career as a mere rebel against the existing order of things in India. His first achievement was, perhaps, the expulsion of Greek garrisons from the Punjab in about 317 BCE. Starting from that point, he became, in a brief span of five years, the emperor of the greater part of India, entering into possession of that scientific frontier "sighed for in vain by his English successors and never held in its entirety even by the Moghul monarchs of the sixteenth and seventeenth centuries."[1] In judging the extent of his conquests, we must remember that India is geographically a continent and the conquest of nearly the whole of this area is no mean achievement. Moreover, as Arrian has noted, a sense of justice prevented the ancient Indian kings from bringing foreign countries under their subjection.[2] They were satisfied by getting their superior power acknowledged by foreign kings, and they performed their *digvijaya* only to this end. Judged by this standard, Candragupta was a successful *digvijayī* inasmuch as he defeated the most powerful foreign king, Seleucus Nicator, who held all Western Asia under his sway. Thus there can be no doubt that Candragupta was a great conqueror.

Candragupta moreover, was, in a real sense, one of those few men who have changed the destinies of nations. But for him, India, with her numerous warring rulers, would have surely fallen a prey to the ambition of the successors of Alexander. He was solely responsible for the redemption of India.

Candragupta, however, was no mere military adven-turer and his greatness does not depend only upon his military feats. The change he brought about in Indian politics was not flickering or temporary. He knew to organize as well as to conquer a vast empire. His organization was so thorough that his empire passed intact at least to his son and grandson. It is, therefore, obvious that he had the will as well as the capacity to organize an empire rarely surpassed in magnitude.

Candragupta has been praised by Indian and foreign authors alike for bestowing prosperity upon his country. Thus, Viśākhadatta, the author of the *Mudrārākṣasa*, has treated him as Deity descended upon earth to restore peace in the country of India troubled by barbarians. Among foreign writers the only one who has accused Candragupta of tyranny is the Roman historian Justin, but his opinion is in contradiction with the earlier account of Megasthenes who everywhere refers to the prosperity of the Indian people.

Candragupta thus distinguished himself in many directions. He was the conqueror of a vast territory, the emancipator of his country, the capable administrator of a great empire, and the harbinger of peace to his people. He is usually considered as the first historical emperor of India. He was undoubtedly the mightiest ruler of his time and one of the most lustrous stars in the firmament of monarchy. It is not easy to embark upon a comparison, but as it is one of the best ways of understanding a person, it would be worthwhile to compare Candragupta with three of the world's most renowned kings — Alexander, Akbar and Napoleon.

Alexander was undoubtedly a great conqueror. We are bound to be dazzled when we recall to mind his wide conquests in a brief space of time — for he died quite young. Yet the truth is that much of what Alexander accomplished had already been planned by his father, Philip, a man of uncommon ability. Alexander had found his field prepared by his father, and thus had no difficulties to face at the outset of his career. In the words of Mr. H.G. Wells "the true hero of the history of Alexander is not so much Alexander as his father Philip."[3] Moreover, the countries conquered by Alexander gained nothing by the change of masters. It may be argued that he had schemes of organization which were frustrated by his early death. But this is hardly borne out by his career. His vanity was insuperable, and his purpose seems to have been to dazzle the world by his valour. His purpose accomplished, he literally drank himself to death. Candragupta, on the other hand, was a man of a different metal. As brave and courageous as Alexander himself, his sole purpose seems to have been to bring peace and honour to his country. He had no advantages of birth and was actually an exile at the outset of his career. He too was a young man when he came on the scene, but in a brief space of time he had not only conquered but thoroughly organized a vast empire, giving all the advantages of a good government to his people. Thus Candragupta has, definitely, better claims for greatness than Alexander.

Akbar, the Moghul monarch, was indeed much like Candragupta. He has often been compared with Aśoka, but in many respects his genius was more allied to that of Candragupta than to that of Aśoka. Like Candragupta he was a man of 'blood and iron.' Like him again, he was a great conqueror and a great administrator. But it must be remembered that Akbar had inherited the resources needed for forming a great empire as against Candragupta who struggled from poverty and exile to power. Moreover, the success of Akbar's administration was more due to the personal qualities of his ministers than to his thorough organization, and even Dr. Vincent Smith has admitted that "Akbar's machine of government never attained the standard of efficiency reached by the Mauryas eighteen or nineteen centuries before his time."[4]

Napoleon certainly was one of the most brilliant figures in history. He resembles Candragupta inasmuch as he also rose by dint of merit, and not by virtue of his birth. In his early youth he dreamt of an independent Corsica, much as Candragupta seems to have dreamt of the independence of his country. But later, Napoleon drifted towards a mere ambition for conquest, and failed to maintain his empire. In fact, his country gained nothing by his splendid exploits. In this respect, he too falls behind the great Maurya.

Candragupta was thus, undoubtedly, an uncommon genius. He was the founder of the greatest Hindu dynasty, to which also belonged the most famous Buddhist and Jain monarchs.[5] His career supplied materials to many poets for writing upon and he is still a popular hero in the modern Indian literature.

Notes

1. V.A. Smith, *Early History of India*, p. 126.
2. McCrindle, *Ancient India : Megasthenes and Arrian, Indika of Arrian* Fragm. IX.
3. Wells, *Outline of History*, p. 344.
4. Smith, *Akbar the Great Mogul*, p. 396.
5. Aśoka and Samprati.

8

Legends of Candragupta

Buddhist

WHILE Buddha yet lived, driven by the misfortunes produced by the wars of (prince) Viḍūḍabha, certain members of the Sākiya line retreating to Himavant discovered a delightful and beautiful location, well watered and situated in the midst of a forest of lofty bo and other trees. Influenced by the desire of settling there, they founded a town at a place where several great roads met, surrounded by durable ramparts, having gates of defence therein, and embellished with delightful edifices and pleasure gardens. Moreover that (city) having a row of building covered with tiles, which were arranged in the pattern of the plumage of peacock's neck, and as it resounded with notes of flocks of *krauñca*s and *mayūra*s it was socalled. From this circumstance these Śākya lords of this town, and their children and descendants, were renowned throughout Jambudvīpa by the title of "Moriya." From this time that dynasty has been called the Moriyan dynasty.

(Candragupta was born in this dynasty.) His mother, the queen consort of the monarch of Moriyanagara, the city before mentioned, was pregnant at the time when a certain powerful provincial *rājā* conquered that kingdom, and put the Moriyan king to death. In her anxiety to preserve the child in her womb, departing for the capital of Pupphapura under the protection of her elder brothers and under disguise she dwelt there. At the completion of the ordinary term of pregnancy giving birth to a son, and relinquishing him to the protection of the Devas, she placed him in a vase and deposited him at the door of a cattle pen. A bull named Cando stationed himself by him, to protect him, in the same manner that Prince Ghoṣa, by the interposition of the Devas was watched over by a bull. In the same manner, also, that the herdsman in the instance of that Prince Ghoṣa repaired to the spot where the bull planted himself, a herdsman, on observing this prince, moved by affection, like that borne to his own child, took charge of and tenderly reared him, and in giving him a name, in reference to his having been watched by the bull Cando, he called him Candagutta, and brought him up. When he had attained an age to be able to tend cattle, a certain wild huntsman, becoming acquainted with, and attached to him, taking him from (the herdsman) to his own dwelling, established him here. He continued to dwell in that village.

Subsequently, on a certain occasion, while tending cattle with other children in the village, he joined them in a game called the "game of royalty." He himself was named Rājā; to others he gave the offices of sub-king, etc. Some being appointed judges, were placed in a judgement hall; some he made officers. Having thus constituted a court of justice, he sat in judgement. On culprits being brought up, regularly inspecting and trying them, on their guilt being clearly proved to his satisfaction, according to the sentence awarded by his judicial ministers, he ordered the officers of the court to chop off their hands and feet. On their replying, "Deva, we have no axes," he answered, "It is the order of Candagutta that ye should chop off their hands and feet, making axes with the horns of goats for blades and sticks for handles. They acting accordingly, on striking with the axe the hands and feet were lopped off. On the same person commanding, "Let them be reunited," the hands and feet were restored to their former condition.

Cāṇakka (a brāhmaṇa), happening to come to that spot, was amazed at the proceedings he beheld. (He had been insulted by King Nanda, for taking revenge against whom he had already taken into confidence a Prince named Pabbato and was in search for a second individual entitled to be raised to sovereign power.) Accompanying (the boy) to the village, and presenting the herdsman with a thousand Kāhāpaṇas, he applied for him; saying, "I will teach your son every accomplishment, consign him to me." Accordingly conducting him to his own dwelling, he encircled his neck with a single fold of woollen cord, twisted with golden thread, worth a lac.

He invested Prince Pabbato, also, with a similar woollen cord. While these youths were living with him, each had a dream which they separately imparted to him. As soon as he heard each (dream) he knew that of these Prince Pabbato would not attain royalty; and that Candagutta would, without loss of time, become paramount monarch in Jambudvīpa. Although he made this discovery, he disclosed nothing to them.

On a certain occasion having partaken of some milkrice prepared in butter, which had been received as an offering at a Brāhmaṇical disputation, retiring from the main road, and lying down in a shady place protected by the deep foliage of trees, they fell asleep. Among them the Āchāriyo awaking first rose; and, for the purpose of putting Prince Pabbato's qualifications to the test, giving him a sword, and telling him, "Bring me the woollen thread on Candagutta's neck, without either cutting or untying it," sent him off. Starting on the mission, and failing to accomplish it, he returned. On a subsequent day, he sent Candagutta on a similar mission. He repairing to the spot where Pabbato was sleeping, and considering how it was to be effected, decided "there is no other way of doing it; it can only be got possession of by cutting his head off." Accordingly chopping his head off, and bringing away the woollen thread, presented himself to the brāhmaṇa, who received him in profound silence. Pleased with him, however, on account of this (exploit), he rendered him in the course of six or seven years highly accomplished, and profoundly learned. Thereafter, on his attaining manhood, deciding "From henceforth this individual is capable of forming and controlling an army," and repairing to the spot where his treasure was buried, and taking possession of, and employing it; and enlisting forces from all quarters, and distributing money among them, and having thus formed a powerful army, he entrusted it to him. From that time throwing off all disguise, and invading the inhabited parts of the country, he commenced his campaign by attacking towns and villages. In the course of their (Cāṇakka and Candagutta's) warfare the population rose *en masse*, and surrounding them and hewing their army with their weapons, vanquished them. Dispersing, they reunited in the wilderness and consulting together, they thus decided, "As yet no advantage has resulted from war; relinquishing military operations, let us acquire a knowledge of the sentiments of the people." Thenceforth, in disguise they travelled about the country. While thus roaming about, after sunset retiring to some town or other, they were in the habit of attending to the conversation of the inhabitants of those places.

In one of these villages, a woman having baked some appalpuwa (pancakes) was giving them to her child, who leaving the edges would only eat the centre. On his asking for another cake, she remarked, "This boy's conduct is like Candagutta's in his attempt to take possession of the kingdom." On his enquiring, "Mother, why, what am I doing, and what has Candagutta done?" "Thou, my boy," (said she,) "throwing away the outside of the cake, eat the middle only. Candagutta also in his ambition to be a monarch, without subduing the frontiers, before he attacked the towns, invaded the heart of the country, and laid towns waste. On that account, both the inhabitants of the town and others, rising, closed in upon him, from the frontiers to the centre, and destroyed his army. *That* was *his* folly."

They on hearing this story of hers, taking due notice thereof, from that time, again raised an army. On resuming their attack on the provinces and towns, commencing from the frontiers, reducing towns, and stationing troops in the intervals, they proceeded in their invasion. After an interval, adopting the same system, and martialling a great army, and in regular course reducing each kingdom and province, then assailing Pāṭaliputra and putting Dhanananda to death, they seized that sovereignty.

Although this had been brought about, Cāṇakka did not at once raise Candagutta to the throne; but for the purpose of discovering Dhanananda's hidden treasure, sent for a certain fisherman (of the river); and deluding him with the promise of raising the *chatta* for him, and having secured the hidden treasure; within a month from that date, putting him also to death, inaugurated Candagutta monarch.[1]

Jain

In a village there lived certain persons as tamers of peacocks. Their headman had a daughter. She gave birth to a son who was named Candragupta. The latter soon grew up into a fine lad.

Candragupta used to play with the boys of the neighbourhood, and give villages and other things to them, as if he were a king. Sometimes, he made the boys act as horses or elephants to ride on them, for the future of a man is often predicted by his previous conduct. Subsequently, on a certain occasion, a brāhmaṇa named Cāṇakya (who had been insulted by King Nanda of Pāṭaliputra, and who was in search of a person who could help him in his vow of revenge) came there, while wandering. He was surprised at the manners of Candragupta, and to test the latter he addressed him thus: "O King let me also have a share in your gifts." Candragupta replied, "O Brahman you are at liberty to choose some for yourself from these village kine. Nobody can dare to withhold what I promise." Cāṇakya, smiling, said, "How shall I take these kine? I fear the cowherds lest they should beat me severely." Candragupta replied, "Do not fear. I allot these cows to thee. The whole earth can be enjoyed by those who are brave." Cāṇakya was struck by his intelligence and asked his playmates as to who he was. The boys told him the way in which, while still in his mother's womb, the boy was promised to be given to an ascetic. Cāṇakya (remembering that it was he himself who had formerly come to the village in the guise of an ascetic) recognized the boy and induced the latter by means of the promise of securing a kingdom, to accompany him. Candragupta too, pleased at the idea of acquiring kingship, agreed to accompany him, and Cāṇakya quickly fled away with the boy like a highwayman. Then, taking hold of his treasures, Cāṇakya arrayed infantry and other forces, for the sake of destroying Nanda. He then besieged the city of Pāṭaliputra on all sides with his forces thus gathered. King Nanda, however, easily defeated the inadequate forces of Cāṇakya. Cāṇakya and Candragupta, thereafter, fled for their lives, for it is said that one should protect oneself at any cost, prosperity being attainable only by preserving one's life. Nanda, on his part, sent some cavaliers to catch Candragupta, for kings cannot tolerate such persons who covet their kingdom. When Nanda returned to his capital triumphant, the citizens celebrated a festival, each contributing his share according to capacity.

One of the cavaliers despatched by King Nanda reached, due to the swiftness of his horse, very near where Candragupta had gone. Cāṇakya, seeing the cavalier from afar and using his quick wit, asked Candragupta to hide himself in the water of the lake that was situated nearby adorned with lotuses. He himself stayed there silent like a *yogī*. The horseman of Nanda quickly came there on his horse, which had the swiftness of wind. He asked Cāṇakya if he had seen some young man recently passing that way. Cāṇakya, pretending to take care lest he should break his silent meditation, pointed his finger towards the water with a hum. The cavalier, in order to draw out Candragupta from water, began to wear his swimming gown, as the dancing girl wears her special petticoat (when she has to perform a dance). Cāṇakya, in the meanwhile, got hold of the cavalier's sword, and cut off the latter's head, as if to offer to the Water-goddess. Then, as he shouted to Candragupta, the latter came out of the water, as the moon rises from the ocean. Then having made Candragupta mount on the horse of the cavalier, Cāṇakya asked him as to what he thought to himself when he was pointed out to the cavalier. Candragupta said that, although he might not understand, he saw nothing but good in what his teacher did. Cāṇakya, on hearing this, thought to himself that such an obedient pupil would never betray him. While they were thus going on, they were again followed by a swift cavalier of Nanda coming like a messenger of Yama. Seeing him, Cāṇakya again asked Candragupta to act as before, which he did. Cāṇakya then persuaded a washerman standing there to believe that King Nanda was angry on his guild, and it was best for him to run away, lest he should be killed by the cavalier that was drawing near. The washerman too, seeing the cavalier coming from afar with drawn sword, believed the truth of Cāṇakya's statement, and fled for his life. Cāṇakya then began to wash the clothes which the washerman had left behind. The cavalier coming near asked Cāṇakya (mistaking him to be a washerman) about the fugitives. The quick-witted Cāṇakya, acting as before, killed that cavalier also. Then Cāṇakya and Candragupta resumed their wanderings. . . .

While thus wandering, Cāṇakya, accompanied by Candragupta, reached a village in the evening, as a bird retires to its nest. In that village, roaming for the sake of alms, he approached the house of a certain old woman, who was serving fresh cooked hot food to her children. There a child, feeling very hungry, got his fingers burnt due to his carelessness. On the child's screaming the old woman remarked, "You are as foolish as Cāṇakya himself." Cāṇakya, overhearing, entered her house and asked the matron the reason for her comparison of the child to Cāṇakya. The old woman replied, "Cāṇakya in his folly, attacked Nanda's capital, before getting control of the frontiers as a result of which he perished. This child, too, put his hand in the centre before slowly eating from the sides and thus got his fingers burnt. Cāṇakya thinking that even a woman was more intelligent than him (and realizing his mistake) went to the Himālayan regions, and there formed alliance with a chief named Parvataka, with a view to secure his help.

One day, Cāṇakya suggested to Parvataka the idea of conquering King Nanda and dividing his kingdom between themselves. Parvataka agreed to this, and then Candragupta, Cāṇakya and Parvataka started to conquer the kingdom of Nanda. On their way, they besieged a town, but could not capture it. Thereupon Cāṇakya entered the town in the disguise of a mendicant. There Cāṇakya saw seven goddesses and thought that it must have been due to them that the town was safe. While he was thinking of the way of removing the images, certain citizens came to him and requested him to predict as to when the town would be free from the invaders. The preceptor of Candragupta replied that so long as the goddesses were there the town would not be secure from enemies. The citizens then quickly removed the images, for there is nothing which a troubled person will not do specially under the influence of a crafty fellow. Chandragupta and Parvataka then retreated at the hint of Cāṇakya, and the citizens became very glad. But the two warriors again came back like a sea-tide and entered the town. Having thus captured this town both the warriors conquered the country of Nanda also; with Cāṇakya as charioteer. Being guided by Cāṇakya, the two heroes at last besieged Pāṭaliputra also with a large army. King Nanda at that time had become destitute of sufficient treasuries and army and counsel and valour, due to his unvirtuous acts, for prosperity retires with virtue. He (being defeated) requested Cāṇakya to grant him a safe retirement, for whoever does not value his life. Cāṇakya also allowed him to leave the city with only one chariot and assured him that none would stop him if he retired as directed. Then King Nanda having taken with him his two wives and a daughter and a sufficient amount of wealth left the city. The daughter of Nanda, at that time was attracted by the appearance of Candragupta and gazed at him unwinked like a goddess. By thus gazing by her side glances the daughter of Nanda proved that she had fallen in love with Candragupta. Nanda too, having understood, asked his daughter to choose her husband according to her will, as was the custom among kings. Accordingly he asked her to get down from his chariot, wishing her well. Being thus asked she got down from that chariot, and began to mount the chariot of Candragupta, as a result of which the spokes were broken, as a sugarcane breaks when pressed by a *yantra*. Candragupta thinking it inauspicious tried to remove her from the chariot. Cāṇakya, however, forbade Candragupta from doing so, telling him that it was a good omen, not only for Candragupta but also for his descendants. Then Candragupta and Parvataka having entered Nanda's palace began to divide the huge wealth of that king. There was also the daughter of Nanda whom the latter Nanda had slowly fed on poison, and Parvataka became so enamoured of her that he treated her like an angel. The preceptor of Candragupta agreed to confer her upon

Parvataka and preparations for marriage were started. But the sweat produced by the nuptial fire caused the transmission of poison into the body of Parvataka (who took the hand of the girl). Being thus afflicted by the agonies of poison his body began to lose energy and he cried to Candragupta to procure a doctor lest he would die. But Cāṇakya whispered to Candragupta to let him alone to die or be cured, for after all the death of Parvataka would clear away a rival of his, without his incurring any sin. Thereafter the Himālayan chief died and the whole empire passed intact to Candragupta. Thus Candragupta became king 155 years after the *mukti* of Srī Mahāvīra.[2]

Hindu

King Nanda was the lord of 99 crores of gold pieces. When he died his body was re-animated by a person proficient in Yoga (with that person's own soul) and, since then, he was known as Yogananda. Śakaṭāla, the minister, hated Yogananda considering him to be an imposter. Yogananda, having known it, punished Śakaṭāla on a false plea. Since then Śakaṭāla became definitely against him.

One day, while brooding on his plan of revenge, he observed a brāhmaṇa digging in a meadow, and asked him the reason for doing that. Cāṇakya, the Brāhmaṇa, replied, "I am rooting out this grass which has hurt my foot." The minister was struck at the reply and regarded that angry firm-minded Brāhmaṇa as the fit person to accomplish the death of Yogananda. He then engaged him by the promise of a reward of one hundred thousand *suvarṇa*s to come and preside at the *śrāddha* which was to be celebrated in the palace of Nanda. Cāṇakya accompanied him to his house and on the appointed day went to preside at the *śrāddha*. Another brāhmaṇa, Subandhu, however, was desirous of getting precedence for himself and Nanda was persuaded by Śakaṭāla to believe that

Subandhu was a fit person to be given precedence. Thereupon Nanda gave orders to remove Cāṇakya from the place which he occupied. Śakaṭāla communicated the orders to Cāṇakya, pleading his own innocence in the matter. Burning with rage, Cāṇakya loosened the knot of his *śikhā*, and took a vow to kill Nanda within seven days, after which alone he would tie his *śikhā* again. On hearing this Nanda was enraged, but Cāṇakya escaped and was secretly sheltered by Śakaṭāla. Thereafter, Cāṇakya being supplied with all materials, practised a magical rite in which he was an adept, and by which on the seventh day Nanda was deprived of life. Śakaṭāla effected the destruction of Yogananda's son Hiraṇyagupta also, and raised Candragupta, the son of the genuine Nanda, on the throne. Cāṇakya became the prince's minister, and Śakaṭāla having obtained the only object of his existence retired to spend his last days in the woods.[3]

European

Seleucus Nicator waged many wars in the east after the partition of Alexander's empire among his generals. He first took Babylon, and then with his forces augmented by victory subjugated the Bactrians. He then passed over into India, which after Alexander's death, as if the yoke of servitude had been shaken off from its neck, had put his prefects to death. Sandrocottus was the leader who achieved their freedom, but after his victory he forfeited by his tyranny all title to the name of liberator, for he oppressed with servitude the very people whom he had emancipated from foreign thraldom. He was born in humble life, but was prompted to aspire to royalty by an omen significant of an august destiny. For when by his insolent behaviour he had offended Nandrus,[4] and was ordered by that king to be put to death, he sought safety by a speedy flight. When he lay down overcome with fatigue and had fallen into a deep sleep, a lion of enormous size approaching the slumberer licked with its tongue the sweat which oozed profusely from his body, and when he awoke, quietly took its departure. It was this prodigy which first inspired him with the hope of winning the throne, and so having collected a band of robbers, he instigated the Indians to overthrow the existing government. When he was thereafter preparing to attack Alexander's prefects, a wild elephant of monstrous size approached him, and kneeling submissively like a tame elephant received him on to its back and fought vigorously in front of the army. Sandrocottus having thus won the throne was reigning over India when Seleucus was laying the foundations of his future greatness. Seleucus having made a treaty with him and otherwise settled his affairs in the east, returned home to prosecute the war with Antigonus.[5]

Notes

1. *Mahāvaṁsa Tīkā*. Translated by Turnour, in his introduction to *Mahāvaṁsa*, LXXVI-LXXXI.
2. *Pariśiṣṭaparvan* of Hemcandra, VIII, 339. Translated by the author.
3. *Kathāsaritsāgara*, I, 5. Translated by the author.
4. *Nandrum* has been here substituted for the common reading *Alexandrum*, which Gutschmid (Rhein. Mus. 12, 261) has shown to be an error.
5. Justin, *De Historiis Philippicis*. Translated by McCrindle, *Invasion of India by Alexander*, pp. 327-28.

Appendix
History of the Sudarśana Lake

Portions of the Junagarh Inscription from *Epigraphia Indica,* Vol. VIII, Edited and Translated by Prof. F. Kielhorn

1. *siddham idaṁ taḍākaṁ sudarśanaṁ gir(i)-nagarādapi(d) (ū) ram a(n)t(a). . . . . (tt) ik-opala-vis-tārāyāmocchraya-niḥsandhi-baddha-dṛ̥ḍha-sar-a-palikatvāt-parvata-pa-*

2. *da-ppratispardhi-suśliṣ(ṭ)a(ba) (ndha) m. . . . (va) jātenākṛ̥trimeṇa setubandhenopapannaṁ suppratividhita-ppraṇālī-parī(v)āha*

3. *miḍhavidhānam ca triskan(dha). . . .n-ādibhir- anuagrahair-mahaty-upacaye vartate. tadidam rājño mahākṣatrapasya sugṛ̥hī-*

4. *tanāmnaḥ svāmi-caṣṭanasya pautra. . . .ḥ putrasya rājno mahākṣatrapasya gurubhir-abhyastanāmno rudradāmno varṣe dvisaptatitam(e) 70 2.*

5. *mārgaśīrṣa-bahula-prat(i). . . .ḥ sṛ̥ṣṭa-vṛ̥ṣṭinā parjanyena ekārṇava-bhūtāyām-iva pṛ̥thi-vyām kṛ̥tāyām girer-ūrjayataḥ suvarnasikatā.*

6. *palāśinī-prabhṛ̥tīnām nadīnām atimātrodvṛ̥ttair-vegaiḥ setum (a) . . . .(ya)mān-anurūpa-pratī-kāramapi-giriśikhara-taru-taṭ-āṭṭalak-opatalpa-dvāra-saranocchraya-vidhvamsinā-yuga-nidhanasadṛ̥-*

7. *śa-paramaghora-vegena vāyunā pramathita-salila-vikṣipta-jarjarīkṛtava (di). . . . .(k)ṣ(i)ptāśma-vṛkṣagulma-latāpratānam ā nadī (ta)lā (d) ity-udghātitam-āsīt. catvāri-hasta-śatā-ni-viṁśad-uttarāṇy-āyateṇa etāvantyeva vistīrṇena.*

8. *panca-saptati hastān-avagāḍhena bhedena nissṛta-sarva-toyam marudhannva kalpam-atibhṛśaṁdurda. . . .(s)y(ā)rthe mauryasya rājñaḥ candrag(u)(pta) (s) (ya)(r) āṣṭriyeṇa (v)aiśyena puṣyaguptena kāritam aśokasya mauryasya (kṛ?) te yavanarājena tuṣ(ā)sphen-ādhiṣṭhāya.*

9. *praṇālībhir-ala(ṅ)kṛta(m). . . . . .*

TRANSLATION

1. This lake Sudarśana, from Girinagara (even a long distance?). . . . . of a structure so well joined as to rival the spur of a mountain, because all its embankments are strong, in breadth, length and height constructed without gaps as they are of stone, (clay). . . . . furnished with a natural dam (formed by?). . . ., and with well provided conduits, drains and means to guard against foul matter, . . . three sections . . . . by . . . . . and other favours is (now) in an excellent condition.

3-6. This same (lake) — on the first of the dark half of Mārgaśīrṣa in the seventy second — 72nd — year of the king, the Mahākṣatrapa Rudradāman whose name is repeated by the venerable, the son of . . . and son's son of the king, the Mahākṣatrapa Lord Caṣṭana the taking of whose name is auspicious. . . . . when by the clouds pouring with rain the earth had been converted as it were into one ocean by the excessively swollen floods of the Suvarṇasikatā, Palāśinī and other streams of mount Urjayat the dam. . . . . though proper precautions (were taken), the water churned by a storm which, of a most tremendous fury befitting the end of a mundane period, tore down hilltops, trees, banks, turrets, upper stories, gates and raised places of shelter — scattered, broke to pieces, (tore apart). . . . with stones, trees, bushes and creeping plants scattered about, was thus laid open down to the bottom of the river.

7. By a breach four hundred and twenty cubits long, just as many broad, (and) seventy-five cubits deep, all the water escaped, so that (the lake), almost like a sandy desert, (became) extremely ugly (to look at).

8. . . . . . for the sake of . . . . ordered to be made by the Vaiśya Puṣyagupta, the provincial governor of the Maurya king Candragupta, adorned with conduits for Aśoka the Maurya by the Yavana king Tuṣāspha while governing, etc.

Bibliography

Ancient Hindu Works

(A) PURĀṆAS

Bhāgavata Purāṇa, Nirnayasagar Press, Bombay, 1929.

Brahmāṇḍa Purāṇa, Venkateshwar Press, Bombay, 1913.

Matsya Purāṇa, Anandashram Sanskrit Series, Poona, 1907.

The Purāṇa Text of the Dynasties of the Kali Age, Ed. F.E. Pargiter, Chowkhamba Sanskrit Series Office, Varanasi, 1962.

Vāyu Purāṇa, Gurumandal Sanskrit Series, Calcutta, 1959.

Viṣṇu Purāṇa with the Com. of Śrīdhara.

(B) OTHER WORKS

Arthaśāstra of Kauṭilya

(1) Ed. R. Shamasastry, Mysore, 1919.

(2) Ed. J. Jolly & R. Schmidt (2 Vols.), Lahore, 1923-24.

(3) Ed. with Com. by T. Ganapati Sastri (3 Vols.), Trivandrum, 1924-25.

(4) Ed. Udayavira Shastri (3 Vols.), Delhi, 1969-70.

(5) Eng. Trans. by Shamasastry (9th ed.), Mysore, 1988.

Āpastamba Dharmasūtra, Kumbakonam, 1895.

Aṣṭādhyāyī of Pāṇinī, Varanasi, 1928.

Daśakumāracarita of Daṇḍin, Ed. M.R. Kale, Delhi, 1966.

Harṣacarita of Bāṇa, Nirnayasagar Press, Bombay, 1946.

Kādambarī of Bāṇa, Nirnayasagar Press, Bombay, 1932.

Kathāsaritsāgara of Somadeva, Nirnayasagar Press, Bombay, 1930.

Mahābhāṣya of Patañjali (3 Vols.), Delhi, 1967.

Manusmṛti, Nirnayasagar Press, Bombay, 1925.

Mṛcchakaṭika of Śūdraka, Poona, 1937.

Mudrārākṣasa of Viśākhadatta with the Com. of Ḍhunḍhirāja, Mrs. Radhabhai Atmaram Sagoon, Bombay, 1900.

Nītisāra of Kāmandaka, Bombay, 1952.

Rājataranginī of Kalhaṇa, Ed. Stein, Bombay, 1892.

Svapnavāsavadattā of Bhāsa, Poona, 1946.

Yājñavalkyasmṛti, Nirnayasagar Press, Bombay, 1926.

Ancient Buddhist Works

Buddhacarita of Aśvaghoṣa, Ed. E.B. Cowell, Oxford, 1893.

Dīpavaṁsa, Ed. & Trans. H. Oldenberg, Williams and Norgate, London, 1879.

Divyāvadāna, Ed. E.B. Cowell & R.A. Neil, The University Press, Cambridge, 1886.

Mahābodhivaṁśa, Ed. S.A. Strong, London, 1891.

Mahāparinibbānasutta, Ed. R.C. Childers, Trubner & Co., 1878.

Mahāvaṁsa

(1) Ed. W. Geiger, London, 1908; Eng. Trans. 1912.

(2) Pt. I Text and Trans. G. Turnour, Colombo, 1887.

Pt. II Text and Trans. L.C. Wijesinha, Colombo, 1909.

Milindapañho, Ed. V. Trenckner, London, 1880; Eng. Trans. T.W. Rhys Davids S.B.E. Oxford, 1890-94.

Ancient Jain Works

Kalpasūtra of Bhadrabāhu, Ed. H. Jacobi, Leipzig, 1879 Eng. Trans. S.B.E. XXII, Oxford, 1892.

Pariśiṣṭaparvan (or *Sthavirāvalīcarita*) of Hemacandra Ed. H. Jacobi (2nd ed.), Calcutta, 1932.

Rājāvalīkathe

Uttarādhyāyana, Ed. J. Charpentier, Upsala, 1922; Eng. Trans. H. Jacobi S.B.E. Oxford, 1895.

Vicāraśreṇī of Merutuṅga

Classical Works (in translation)

McCrindle, J.W., *The Invasion of India by Alexander the Great as Described by Arrian Q. Curtius, Diodorus, Plutarch, and Justin*, AMS Press, New York, 1972.

McCrindle, J.W., *Ancient India as Described in Classical Literature*, Oriental Books Reprint Corporation, New Delhi, 1979.

McCrindle, J.W., *Ancient India as Described by Megasthenes and Arrian*, Today and Tomorrow's Printers & Publishers, New Delhi, 1972.

Strabo, *Geography*, Eng. Trans. by H.C. Hamilton and W. Falconer, London, 1854-57.

Modern Works

Aiyangar, S.K., *Beginnings of South Indian History*, Madras, 1918.

Altekar, A.S., *Education in Ancient India*, Nand Kishore, Varanasi, 1965.

Altekar, A.S., *Position of Women in Hindu Civilization*, Motilal Banarsidass, Delhi, 1959.

Asiatic Researches, Vol. IV, Bengal Military Orphans Press, Calcutta, 1788-1839.

Bandopadhyaya, N.C., *Kauṭilya*, Calcutta, 1927.

Barnett, L.D. *Antiquities of India*, London, 1913.

Bhandarkar, D.R., *Aśoka* (4th ed.), University of Calcutta, Calcutta, 1969.

Bhandarkar, R.G., *Vaisnavism, Saivism and Minor Religious Systems*, Strassburg, 1913.

Bhargava, P.L., *Founders of India's Civilization*, Asian Humanities Press, Berkeley, California, 1992.

Brown, Percy, *Indian Architecture*, D.B. Taraporevala Sons & Co., Bombay, 1976.

Bühler, G., *The Indian Sect of the Jainas*, Trans. J. Burgess, Luzac & Co., London, 1903.

Codrington K. de B., *Ancient India from the Earliest Time to the Guptas*, E. Benn Limited, London, 1926.

Coomaraswamy, A.K., *History of Indian and Indonesian Art*, London, 1927.

Davids, T.W. Rhys, *Buddhist India*, Motilal Banarsidass, Delhi, 1971.

Dikshitar, V.R.R., *The Mauryan Polity*, Madras, 1932.

Epigraphia Indica, Vol. VIII, New Delhi : Director-General, Archaeological Survey of India.

Fergusson, J., *A History of Indian and Eastern Architecture*, London, 1910.

Gopal, Lallanji, *Chandragupta Maurya*, Trans. O.P. Tandon, National Book Trust, New Delhi, India, 1969.

Gopal, M.H., *Mauryan Public Finance*, London, 1935.

Ghoshal, U.N., *History of Hindu Political Theory*, London, 1923.

Ghoshal, U.N., *Contributions to the History of the Hindu Revenue System*, Calcutta, 1930.

Havell, *Aryan Rule in India*, London.

Hultzsch, E., *Inscriptions of Asoka*, Indological Book House, Delhi, 1969.

Jayaswal, K.P., *Hindu Polity : A Constitutional History of India in Hindu Times*, Bangalore Print. and Pub. Co., Bangalore, 1967.

Keith, A.B., *A History of Sanskrit Literature*, Oxford, 1961.

Keith, A.B., *The Religion and Philosophy of the Vedas*, Harvard, 1925.

Keith, A.B., *The Sanskrit Drama*, Oxford, 1970.

Kern, *Manual of Indian Buddhism*, Strassburg, 1896.

Konow, Sten, *Kautilya Studies*, Delhi, 1975.

Kramrisch, Stella, *Indian Sculpture*, Calcutta, 1933.

Law, N.N., *Studies in Ancient Hindu Polity*, Calcutta, 1914.

Macdonell, A.A., *A History of Sanskrit Literature*, Motilal Banarsidass, Delhi, 1986.

Macphail, J.M., *Asoka*, Heritage of India Series, Association Press, Calcutta, 1918.

Majumdar, R.C., *Corporate Life in Ancient India* (3rd edn.), Firma K.L. Mukhopadhyay, Calcutta, 1969.

Majumdar, R.C. and Pusalkar, A.D. (Ed.), *History and Culture of the Indian People Vol. II — The Age of Imperial Unity*, Bombay, 1951.

Masson-Oursel, P., Helen de Willman-Grabowska, Philippe Stern, *Ancient India and Indian Civilization*, Anmol Publications, Delhi, 1986.

Mookerji, R.K., *Asoka*, London, 1928.

Mookerji, R.K., *Indian Shipping : A History of the Sea-borne Trade and Maritime Activity of the Indians from the Earliest Times*, Orient Longmans, Bombay, 1957.

Mookerji, R.K., *Local Government in Ancient India*, Motilal Banarsidass, Delhi, 1958.

Mookerji, R.K., *Chandragupta Maurya and His Times* (4th edn.), Motilal Banarsidass, 1966.

Nilakanta Sastri, K.A., *Age of the Nandas and Mauryas* (2nd edn.), Delhi, 1967.

Oldenberg, *Buddha*, London, 1882.

Rapson, E.J., *Ancient India from the Earliest Times to the First Century* CE, Cambridge, 1914.

Rapson, E.J. (Ed.), *The Cambridge History of India*, Vol. I, Cambridge, 1922.

Raychaudhuri, H.C., *Materials for the Study of the Early History of the Vaishnava Sect*, Calcutta, 1920.

Raychaudhuri, H.C., *Political History of Ancient India* (5th edn.), Calcutta, 1950.

Ray, Nihar Ranjan, *Maurya and Sunga Art*, Calcutta, 1945.

Rice, B.L., *Mysore and Coorg from Inscriptions*, Asian Educational Services, New Delhi, 1986.

Samaddar, J.N., *The Glories of Magadha*, K.P. Jayaswal Research Institute, Patna, 1990.

Smith, V.A., *Asoka, the Buddhist Emperor of India*, Low Price Publications, Delhi, 1990.

Smith, V.A., *Early History of India* (4th edn.), Oxford, 1924.

Smith, V.A., *History of Fine Art in India and Ceylon* (2nd edn.), Oxford, 1930.

Spooner, D.B., *Excavations at Pataliputra*, Annual Report Archaeological Survey of India, 1912-13.

Stevenson, *The Heart of Jainism*, Oxford, 1915.

Subba Rao, N.S., *Economic and Political Conditions in Ancient India*, Mysore, 1911.

Waddell, L.A., *Report on the Excavations at Pataliputra*, Sanskaran Prakashak, Delhi, 1975.

Watters, T., *On Yuan Chwang's Travels in India*, Munshiram Manoharlal, Delhi, 1973.

Winternitz, M., *History of Indian Literature* (2 Vols. Eng. Trans. S. Ketkar 2nd edn.), New Delhi, 1972.

Index

Abhidhammapiṭaka, 77

Abhisāra, 28

Abhiṣeka, 6, 46n

Achaemenian,
  empire, 108

Adhyakṣas (superintendents), 54

Administration,
  military, 55-7
  municipal, 57-9
  rural, 59-61
  provincial, 61-2
  finance, 62-3
  law and justice, 64-7

Adrastai (Adhṛṣṭas), 29

Afghanistan, 41, 50, 62

Agalassoi, 30

Agastya, 96n

Agni, 72

Agnihotra, 72

Agrammes (Augrasainya), 25

Agriculture, 60, 91

Aiyangar, S.K., 40

Ajanta, 106

Ajātaśatru, 2-7, 12n, 17-20, 76

Ājīvikas, 71, 78-9

Akbar, 9, 51, 62, 115-6

Akesines (Asiknī),
  river, 28

Alexander of Epirus, 6

Alexander the Great, 1, 5, 10, 21, 25,
  Indian campaigns of-, 26- 31, 33,
    36-8, 40, 46n, 54, 73- 4, 76,
    108, 114-5, 127-8

Amātyas,
  eighteen kinds of-, 51

Ambaṣṭha, 95n

Ambaṣṭhas, 30

Āmbhi, 27

Āndhra, 50

Andrae, 67n

Androkottos (Candragupta), 40,
  46n

Aṅga, 15, 17, 101

Aṅguttara Nikāya, 15, 19, 77

Antapāla, 53

Antarvaṁśika, 52

Antigonus Gonatus, 6

Antiochus Theos, 6

Anuruddha, 7, 19
Aornos, 27
Āpastamba Dharmasūtra, 96n
Appian, 10, 41
Arabian Sea, 31
Arachosia, 41
Architecture, 107
Aria, 41
Ariana, 41
Aristobulus, 10
Aristotle on slavery, 102
Arjuna, 75, 95n, 96n
Arrian, 10, 42, 56, 63, 82, 88, 90, 93, 95, 100, 113
Arthaśāstra, 9:
  age of-, 11-2;42
  methods of administration in, 51-67;69n
  marriage and divorce in, 86-7
  slavery in, 87-8
  vices of the aristocratic classes, 90
  coin in, 90
  crops mentioned in, 91
  famine relief measures mentioned in, 92
  industries in, 92-3
  trade in, 93-4
  critical estimate of-, 102-3
  resemblance of-, with *Kāmasūtra*, 103
Artisans,
  as servents of state, 58;
  as a class of Indian population, 83
Arundhatī, 96n
Ārya,
  Kauṭilya's definition of-, 102-3
Āryaka, 22
Aryan, 16, 80, 84, 87, 88
Āryas,
  prohibition of the enslavement of-, 102-3
Āryāvarta, 100, 103
Asiknī, (Chenab): river, 28
Aśmaka, 16, 24
Aśmakas, 23
Aśoka, 6, 7, 9, 12, 26, 32n, 33-4, 45n, 46n, 47n, 50-3, 61-2, 67n, 71, 77, 79, 89, 96n, 101, 104, 106, 115, 131
Āśramas, 84
Assakenoi, 26
Assam, 67n
Aṣṭādhyāyī, 32n
Astrology, 110, 111n
Aśvaghoṣa, 3,16
Āśvalāyanas, 26-8
Aśvamedha (horse sacrifice), 72-3
Augrasainya, 25
Avadh, 16
Avantī, 4, 16-7, 20, 23-4
Avantis, 17

Babylon, 31, 40, 94, 127
Bactrians, 127
Balibandha, 105

Baluchistan, 41, 50, 62

Bāṇa, 8, 21, 102

Banaras, 92, 104

Bandhupālita, 7, 9

Bappa, 46n

Basarh-Bakhira pillar, 106

Bāveru Jātaka, 94

Beas, river, 24, 29

Bengal, 24, 49, 67n, 92

Besnagar, 76, 106

Bhaddasāla, 39

Bhadrā, 19

Bhadrabāhu, 10, 44, 78-9, 103-4

Bhagavadgītā, 75

Bhāgavata(s), 76, 109

Bhāgavata Purāṇa, 8-9

Bhaggas, 16

Bhakti, 75

Bhandarkar, D.R., 6, 53

Bharata (King), 41

Bharata (author of *Nāṭyaśāstra*), 103

Bhārata war, 16

Bhāsa, 18, 22

Bhattiya, 12n, 16

Bhṛgu, 101

Bihar, 19, 101

Bihar (south), 16

Bimbisāra, 2, 4-6, 12n, 16-8, 22, 32n

Bindusāra, 6, 8, 34, 44, 45n, 49-50, 67n

Boards,
- for military administration, 55-7
- for municipal administration, 57-9

Bow, Indian, 56

Brachmanes, 43, 73, 75, 77-8

Brahmacārin, 84

Brahmadatta, 17

Brāhmaṇa(s),
- repudiation of their King's humiliating treaty with Alexander by, 31; 34, 71
- interest in spiritual knowledge of a particular class of-, 72-3
- Megasthenes' description of-, 73-5
- identification of the Brachmanes with-, 77
- *Nirgranthas* called by Megasthenes as, 78
- occupations permitted in time of need for, 80
- as belonging to Megasthenes' class of philosophers, 81
- as generals of army and other high officers, 83-4
- as students and house holders, 84-6
- except at sacrifices wine not taken by, 90

Brāhmaṇas, 99, 111n

Brahmāṇḍa Purāṇa, 7-9

Brāhmī script, 101

Breloer, B., 11

Bṛhadratha,
Maurya, 8-9, 96n
Paurava-Bhārata, 16
Bṛhadrathas, 17
Bṛhatkathā, 10,34
Bṛhatkathāmañjarī, 9
Buddha,
date of the *nirvāṇa* of-, 1-2; 16, 18, 20, 34
as founder of a new religion, 76
mention of-, as Boutta by clemens of Alexandria, 77-8; 117
Buddhacarita, 12n
Buddhas, 32n
Buddhism, 76-7, 80, 109
Buddhist Council,
first, 18
second, 21,76-7
Bulis, 16

Cakravartin, 45, 47n
Calcutta, 106
Calingae, 67n
Campā, 17
Cāṇakya,
as a patronymic, 11
as adviser of Candragupta, 32
helper of Candragupta, 36-7
prime minister of Candragupta, 39
guide of Candragupta, 45;84
family, life and work of-, 101-3; 110, 119 ff
Cāṇakka = Cāṇakya, q.v
Candragupta,
identification with Sandrakottos, 1
discussion of the date of the accession of-, 5-7
chronology of the successors of-, 7-9
sources of the history of-, 9-12
Kalinga not included in the dominion of-, 26
factors which contributed to the success of-, 31-2
ancestry of-, 33-6
date of the birth of-, 36
early life of-, 36-7
meeting of-, with Alexander, 37
conquest of the Punjab and Sindh by, 37-8
defeat of the Nandas by, 38-9
coronation of-, 39
defeat of the plot of Malayaketu by, 39
inclusion of Saurāṣṭra in the dominions of-, 39
conquest of the Deccan by, 40
date and account of the defeat of Seleucus Necator by, 40-1
Megasthenes sent as ambassador in the court of, 41
description of Pāṭaliputra the capital of-, 42
description of the palace of-, 42-3, 107-8
personal life of-, 43-4
personal supervision of justice by, 43

fondness of-, for sports, 43-4
religion of-, 44
family of-, 44-5
earning of the title of cakravartin by, 45
Sabhā of-, 47n
extend of the empire of-, 49-50
Justin on the oppression of-, 52
the number of generations of kings that ruled in India up to the accession of-, 100
achievements of-, 113-15
comparison of-, with other great monarchs of the world, 115-6
Buddhist legends of-, 117-21
Jain legends of-, 121-6
Hindu legends of-, 126-27
European legends of-, 127-8
Sudarśana lake built in the reign of-, 131

Canton, 1

Cārvāka:
philosophy, 100

Caṣṭana, 130

Caste,
in the Maurya age, 80 ff

Caturaṅga (chess), 108

Cedi, 15

Ceylon, 106

Chāndogya Upaniṣad, 75

Chenab,
river, 28-30

Chess, 108

China, 94

Chittor, 46n

Cities:
Indian, Arrian's description of-, 91

Cleisobora, 76

Clemens of Alexandria, 77

Cola, 50

Corsica, 116

Counsellors and assessors,
as a class of Indian population, 83

Curtius, 10, 21, 23-5, 76

Cyavana, 96n

Cyrene, 6

Dandamis, 73-5

Daṇḍin, 11

Darius I, 108

Darśaka, 2-5, 18-9, 32n

Dāsa(s), 88

Daśaratha, 7-9, 47n, 79

Daśona, 8

Dauvārika, 52

Deccan, 40

Delhi, 101

Devakī, 75

Devardhi, 104

Devavarman, 8-9

Dhammapada, 77

Dhammasuttas, 76

Dhana Nanda, 39, 121

Dharmaśāstra(s), 67, 80
Dharmasthīya, 64
Dharmasūtras, 86, 99
Dhoti, 96n
Ḍhunḍhirāja, 46n
Didarganj, 106
Digambara (sect of Jains), 95n
Dīgha Nikāya, 12n, 77
Digvijaya, conquest of countries in all directions, 41
Diodora, 44
Diodorus, 10, 25, 32n, 62, 82
Dionysos, 100
Dīpavaṁsa, 2, 10
Divorce,
  Kauṭilya's views on, 87
Divyāvadāna, 10, 25, 34, 45n
Drāmila (Tamil), epithet of Cāṇakya, 101
Dress, Indian, Arrian's description of-, 88
Dupatta, 96n
Durdharā, 44

Egypt, 6, 81-2
  trade with-, 94, 109
Egyptians, 109
Ekbatana, 42, 107, 111n
Empedocles, 109
English law, 69n
Envoys,
  three kinds of-, 54

Epirus, 6
Erannaboas (Hiraṇyavāha), 42
Espionage, 63-4
Eudemos, 5, 38

Females,
  acting as guards, 43
Fighting men,
  as a class of Indian population, 83
Fines,
  three kinds of-, 66
Finance, 62 ff
Foreigners,
  board in charge of-, 58

Gaṇpati Sastri, 11
Gandhāra, 16, 27, 101, 110
Gaṅgā,
  river, 19, 95
Gangaridae, 24, 49
Ganges (Gaṅgā),
  river, 42
Gārgī Saṁhitā, 8, 111n
Gaya, 16
Gedrosia, 41
Ghasundi,
  inscription, 75
Ghora Āṅgirasa, 75
Girinagara, 130
Girnar, 12
Girivraja, 16-7, 20

Glaucukāyanas, 28
Glauganikae, 28
Godāvarī, river, 24, 26
Gopala, 22
Gotra (family name), 13n
Greece, 26, 75, 108
Greek (language), 108
Greeks, 25, 27-30, 58, 73, 76, 88, 96n, 108-10, 111n
Gṛhastha, 84
Gṛhya Sūtras, 99

Haihayas, 23
Hanuman, 95n
Harṣacarita, 8, 21
Haryana, 26, 101
Haryaṅka dynasty, 3-4, 16, 20
Hāthigumpha,
  inscription of Kharavela, 24
Haviryajñas, sacrifices with oblation of meat or food offering, 72
Hazara, 28
Heliodorus, 76, 109
Hemachandra, 10, 12n, 44, 79, 104, 110n
Herakles, 75-6
Herat, 41
Herdsmen and hunters,
  as a class of Indian population, 82-3
Hieun-Tsang, 25
Himalayas, 24, 47n
Himavant (Himalaya), 117
Hindukush, 26
Hiraṇyagupta, 127
Hiraṇyavāha, river, 42
Husbandmen,
  as a class of Indian population, 82
Hydaspes (Vitastā),
  river, 27
Hydraotes (Irāvatī),
  river, 29
Hylobioi (Forest dwellers), 77
Hyphasis (Vipāś),
  river, 29

Ikṣvāku dynasty, 16
Ikṣvākus, 23
Images,
  worship of-, 76
Indian Ocean, 47n
Indians,
  morals of-, 89
Indika, 10, 33
Indo-Aryan, 15, 33
Indra, 72
Indrapālita, 7, 9
Indus (Sindhu),
  river, 26-31, 38, 40
Ionians, 109
Irāvatī (Ravi),
  river, 29
Irrigation, 61
Ivory work, 93

Jacobi, H., 11, 46n, 104
Jainism, 44, 78
Jains, 32n, 92
Jamadagni, 96n
Jambudvīpa, 39, 40, 46n, 117, 119
Jammu & Kashmir, 28
Janamejaya, 15-6
Janapadas, 68n
Jātakas, 93, 107
Jayaswal, K.P., 11, 68n
Jews, 75
Jhelum,
  river, 27-9, 46n
Jinas, 32n
Jñāna, 72
Jobenes (Yamunā),
  river, 76
Johnston, E.H., 11
Jolly, 11
Jones, Sir William, 1
Junagarh,
  inscription, 18
Justin, 10, 35, 37-8, 46n, 52, 114

Kabul, 41
Kākavarṇi, 4-5, 12n, 21, 23
Kālamas, 16
Kālāśoka, 7, 21, 23, 76-7
Kālāśoka's sons, 7
Kalbappu hill, 44
Kalhaṇa, 67n
Kaliṅga, 24-5, 32n, 50, 67n, 92
Kaliṅgas, 23
Kalpasūtra,
  of Bhadrabāhu, 10, 34, 104
Kāmandaka, 103
Kāmasūtra, 103
Kāmboja, 16-57
Kaṁsavadha, 105
Kandahar, 41
Kaṇṭaka śodhana,
  courts, 64-5
Kāṇva,
  Kings, 34, 45n
Karma, 72
Karmāntika, 53
Karnataka, 62, 78
Kāśeyas, 23
Kāśī, 15, 17-8, 20, 23-4, 101
Kashmir, 49, 62, 67n
Kaśyapa,
  gotra, 34
Kathaioi, 29
Kaṭhas, 29
Kathāsaritsāgara, 9, 25, 32n
Kaṭha Upaniṣad, 72
Kathāvatthu, 77, 104
Kathiawar, 49, 61
Kathmandu, 67n
Kātyāyana, 24
Kātyāyanī, 96n
Kauśāmbī,
  city, 16

Kauṭili,
  variant of Kauṭilya, 13n
Kauṭilya (family name of Cāṇakya):
  author of *Arthaśāstra*, 9, 11
  preference of-, for a highborn king, 34
  precept, of-, on the king's time table, 43
  policy of conciliation towards conquered kings advocated by, 50
  view of-, on the king's duty towards his subjects, 51
  kinds of envoys recognized by, 54
  implementation of ideas of the *Arthaśāstra* by, 54
  reference to the chiefs managing the four wing of the army by, 55
  mines regarded as source of treasury by, 60
  recognition of the superiority of king's edicts to other sources of law by, 64
  more rational and liberal han the authors of the ancient texts on sacred law, 65
  mention of compensation for stolen property by, 66-7
  mention by, of occasions when prisoners are set free, 67
  lack of enthusiasm about sacrifices on the part of-, 73
  duties of four castes according to, 79
  king's ownership of land not recognized by, 82
  mention of divorce by, 87
  slavery for Āryas prohibited by, 87
  mention of a government mint by, 90
  China silk mentioned by, 94
  mention of some of the characters of the epics by, 99
  mention of Sāṅkhya and Yoga by, 100
  liberalism of-, in respect of slavery and position of the Śūdras, 102
Keith, A.B., 11
Kekaya, 27, 101
Kerala, 50
Keśava, 76
Khārvela,
  Hathigumpha inscription of-, 24
Khuddaka Nikāya, 77
Kipling, Ruyard, 32n
Koliyas, 16
Kos, 69n
Kosala, 15-20, 23-4, 101, 106
Kosalā Devī, 17-8
Koṭila, 13n
Kṛṣṇa, 75-6, 95n, 96n
Kṣatrapa, 108
Kṣatraujas, 2-3, 5, 16, 17
Kṣatriya(s), 24, 30:
  Mauryas regarded as, 34
  duties of-, 80,82-4
  Gāndharva and *Rākṣasa* marriages approved for, 86; 96n

Kṣemadharman, 2, 3, 5, 16
Kṣemajit, 12n, 16
Kṣemendra, 9
Kṣudrakas, 30
Kukuras, 50
Kumāras, 62
Kumrahar, 107
Kuṇāla, 7-8
Kunar,
    river, 26
Kuru(s), 15-6, 23-4, 50, 101
Kusumapura, 19, 107

Lakṣmaṇa, 95n
Land revenue, 62
Lauria Nandangarh, 46n
Law,
    four kinds of-, 64
Law courts,
    procedure of-, 65
Leather worker, 93
Licchavis, 50
Lokāyata,
    philosophy, 100
Lopāmudrā, 96n

Macdonell, A.A., 109
Macedonia, 6, 26, 82
Machaevelli, 110n
Madhyadeśa, 101
Madhya Pradesh, 76
Madra(s), 50-1, 101
Madura, 92
Magadha, 2,4:
    chronology of the kings of-, 4-5; 15
    definition and early history of-, 16
    history of the Haryaṅka dynasty of-, 16-20
    history of the Śiśunāga dynasty of-, 20-1
    history of the Nanda dynasty of-, 21-6
    Candragupta's early life in and revolt against the kingdom of-, 36-7
    Candragupta's conquest of-, 38-9; 78-9, 101, 106
Magus, 6
Mahābhārata, 99
Mahābhāṣya, 47n
Mahābodhivaṁsa, 10, 23
Mahājanapadas, 15
Mahākaśyapa, 18
Mahākosala, 17
Mahākṣatrapa, 130
Mahāmātras, 52
Mahānandin, 2-5, 19, 21-3
Mahāpadma,
    epithet of Nanda q.v.
Mahāpadmapati,
    epithet of Nanda, 23
Mahāparinibbāna Sutta, 10, 33
Mahāsaṅghikas, 77

Mahāsena, 17

Mahasthan,
    inscription, 67n

Mahāvaṁsa, 2, 6, 10, 12n, 17, 19, 20, 23, 34, 39, 40, 47n, 49

Mahāvaṁsaṭīkā, 10, 12n, 34-5, 37, 46n

Mahāvīra, 1
    date of the demise of-, 2;12n
    founder of Jainism, 18, 78; 79, 103, 126

Maithilas, 23

Maitreyī, 96n

Majjhima Nikāya, 12n, 77

Makkhali Gosāla, 79

Makran, 31

Mālavas, 30

Malayaketu, 39, 50, 67n

Malla(s), 15-6, 50

Malwa,
    western, 17
    eastern, 17, 23-4, 62

Mandanis, 73

Māndhātṛ, 41

Mantrin, 52

Mantripariṣad, 53

Manu, 100

Marriages,
    different kinds of-, 86

Maśakāvatī, 26

Maskarin, 79

Massaga, 26

Mathurā, 76, 106

Matsya, 16, 101

Matsya Purāṇa, 2-4, 7-9, 12, 13n

Maudgaliputra Tiṣya, 104

Maurya empire, 1, 5
    main cause of rise of-, 32, 40
    Pāṭaliputra the metro polis of-, 42, 47n
    administration of-, 51
    bureaucracy, 54
    military administration of-, 55
    rural adminstration of-, 59

Maurya kings,
    chronology of-, 7-9

Mauryaputra, 34

Mauryas, 2
    Kṣatriya origin of-, 33-4 advance of-,
    up to Tinnevelly district in early time, 40
    army of-, 55
    introduction of image worship by, 63, 76
    high standard of efficiency of the government of-, 116

Max-Muller, 1

McCrindle, J.W., 10

Medicine,
    science of-, 100

Megasthenes,
    author of *Indika*, 10
    and Kauṭilya, 11
    sent as ambassador to the Maurya court, 41
    on the city of Pāṭaliputra, 42
    on the kingdom of Kaliṅga, 50

on the strength of Candragupta's army and war office, 55-7
on municipal administration, 57-9
on rural administration, 59
on usages of the Indians for prevention of famine, 60-1
on irrigation, 61
on the absence of written law in India, 64
on the hearing of cases by the king, 65
on the efficiency of criminal administration, 66
on the prevalence of the performance of sacrifices among aristocratic classes, 72
on the employment of Brāhmaṇas by the aristocratic classes for the performance of sacrifices, 72
on the opinion of Brāhmaṇas regarding the beginning of the world and other allied matters, 73
on the Brāhmaṇas and the Jews, 75
on worship of Herakles, i.e. Kṛṣṇa in Mathurā, 75-6
on the Buddhist Śramaṇas, 77-8
on the *Nirgranthas*, 78
on the seven classes of Indian population, 81-4
on the Brāhmaṇa student and householder, 84-6
on marriage among Indians, 86-7
on slavery in India, 87
on the love of finery by the Indians, 89
on the abstinence of the Brāhmaṇas from wine, 90
on the production of crops in India, 91
on metals and metal work in India, 92-3
on Dionysos i.e. Manu and the number of generations of kings that ruled between him and Candragupta, 100
on the skill of Indians in the arts, 105
on the art of sculpture in India, 106
on Indian architecture with reference to the palace of Candragupta, 107
on the comparison of Mauryan palace with the palaces of Susa and Ekbatana, 111n
Justin's accusation of Candragupta contradicted by the account of-, 114

Menander, 110

Metals,
known in the Maurya age, 92-3

Methora (Mathurā), 76

Meyer, J.J., 11

Milinda, 110

Milindapañho, 39

Mīmāṁsā,
philosophy, 100

Mining industry, 92-3
Mithilā, 18, 23-4
Mleccha(s), 87, 96n, 102
Mookerji, Radha Kumud, 51
Moris, 34, 46n
Moriya(s) (Pali form of Mauryas) 16, 34
ruling clan of Pipphalivana, 35
connection of the name with Moras or peacocks, 35, 46n, 117
Moriyanagara, 117
Mṛcchakaṭikam, 22
Mudrārākṣasa, 9, 34, 39, 46n, 50, 67n, 114
Mughal emperors, 62
Mughal empire, 9
Mukhyas, 53-4
Mukti (emancipation), 126
Mulnamar, 40
Muṇḍa, 7, 19-20, 22-3
Munis, 81
Murā, 34, 46n
Music, 105
Musicanus, 31
Mysore, 40, 44, 49

Nāgadāsaka, 7, 19-20, 32n
Nāgaraka, 57
Nagaravyāvahārika, 53
Nagarjuni hill caves, 7
Nanaghat inscription, 75
Nanda (Mahāpadma), 4, 5, 12n
origin of-, 21-3
conquests of-, 24; 25, 31, 35, 126
Nanda empire, 5, 26, 29, 31, 38
Nandas, 4-7, 25-6, 34, 36-7, 39, 49, 51, 55, 76
Nandivardhana, 2-5, 19
Napoleon, 115-6
Nārada,
on the validity of royal decree, 64
Naṭasūtras, 105
Nāṭaśāstra, 103
Nau Nand Dehra, 24
Nāyaka (chief of police), 53
Nearchus, 10, 88, 96n
Nepal, 46n, 49, 67n, 92
Nicanor, 26, 28
Nigalisagar, 67n
Nilakanta Sastri, 11, 54
Nirgrantha(s), 71, 78-9
Niṣādas, 82
Nirvāṇa (emancipation), 1
Nītisāra, 103
Nyāya,
philosophy, 100

Onesicritus, 10
Orissa, 24
Overseers,
as a class of Indian population, 83

Ox races, 43
Oxycanus, 31

Pabbato = Parvataka q.v.
Padmāvatī, 18-9
Painting, 105-6
Pakṣa (group of families claiming a common ancestor), 13n
Palace,
 Maurya, 42-3, 107-8
Pālaka, 22
Palāśinī,
 river, 130
Pāli, 101, 104
Palibothra,
 Palimbothra, 42
Paṇa(s), 52-3, 66, 68n, 87, 90
Pāñcāla(s), 15, 16, 23-4, 51, 101
Panchayats, 64
Pāṇḍya, 50
Pāṇini, 27, 29, 75, 99, 101, 105, 109
Pargiter, F.E., 4, 8
Pariśiṣṭaparvan, 10, 12n, 21-2, 32n, 35, 37, 46n
Parivrājaka, 84
Parkham, 106
Paropanisadiae, 41
Parthalis,
 capital of Calingae, 67n
Parvataka, 36, 39, 46n, 50, 119, 124-6
Pāṭaliputra,
 date of the foundation of, 19; 20-22, 35
 description of-, 42; 44
 the way of the administration of-, 57-9
 the efficiency of the administration of-, 66
 population of-, 66
 council of the *Nirgrantha* monks at, 79
 the royal road connecting other big cities with-, 95
 a centre of education, 104; 107, 111n, 121, 125
Patan, 67n
Patañjali, 47n, 63, 76, 105
Patna, 16, 19, 93
Pattala, 31
Pauras, 68n
Paurava (1) 27-9, (2) 29
Paurava-Bhārata(s), 15-6, 23
Pauravyāvahārika (city magistrate), 53
Peithon, 31, 38
Penal code, 66-7
Persepolis, 108
Persia, 49, 108-9
Persian language, 108
Persian empire, 26, 41, 108
Persians, 108
Philip,
 father of Alexander, 26, 115
 officer, 27-30, 38

Philosophers,
as a class of Indian population, 81
Phrygia, 40
Pimprama, 29
Piṅgala, 99
Pipphalivana, 34-5
Plato, 73
Pliny, 10, 41, 55
Plutarch, 10, 25, 32n, 37, 40, 49
Pollock, Sir Frederic, 103
Porus, 27, 38, 46n, 76
Prācī, 37, 49
Prācya, 24, 101
Pradeṣṭṛ (district officer), 53, 65
Pradyota, 17-8, 20, 22
Pradyotas, 4, 20
Prākṛt,
language of the common people, 100
three main varieties, 101
greatest author of-, 103-4
Praśāstṛ (information officer), 52
Prasenajit, 17-8
Prassians, 42
Prassii, 24-5, 37, 49
Prayāga, 15-6
Precious stones, 92-3
Preya, 72
Prisoners,
set free on certain occasions, 67
Pṛthvīrāj, 96n
Ptolemy Philadelphus, 6
Pulaka, 17
Punch, 28
Punjab, 5, 27, 30-2, 37-8, 46n, 62, 113
Pupphapura, 117
Purāṇa(s), 2-4, 6, 8-9, 16-7, 19- 25, 34, 46n, 47n, 99, 100
Purohita (high priest), 152
Puṣkalāvatī, 26-7, 95
Puṣyagupta,
governor of Candragupta in Surāṣṭra, 61-2, 84, 131
Puṣyamitra Śuṅga, 96n
Pythagoras, 109

Raghu, 41
Raichur, 62
Rājagṛha, 17
Rajasthan, 26, 101
Rājasūya (ceremony of the "royal consecration"), 72
Rājāvalīkathe, 44
Rajput clan of Moris, 34
Rākṣasa (minister of King Nanda), 39
Rāma, 16, 95n
Rāmāyaṇa, 16, 99
Rāṣṭrapāla (governor), 53, 62
Rāṣṭriya, 62
Ravi,
river, 29-30
Rawalpindi, 27

Royal road, 95
Raychaudhury, H.C., 25
Ray, Nihar Ranjan, 111n
Ṛcīka, 96n
Reṇukā, 96n
Ṛgveda, 101
Rhys Davids, T.W., 105
Ripuñjaya, 16
Roads, 59, 94-5
Ṛṣis, 96n
Rudradāman, 12, 39, 49-51, 61, Junagarh inscription of-, 129-31
Rukmiṇī, 96n
Rummindei, 67n

Sabhā, 68n
Sacrifices, 43-4, 72-3
Sahalya (Sahālin, Sukalpa, Sumālya), eldest son of Nanda, 24-5, 31
Śakaṭāla, 126-7
Śākya(s), 16, 34-5, 117
Śāliśuka, 8-9
Samāhartṛ (collector-general), 52, 62
Sāmaveda, 105
Sambos, 31
Samiti, 68n
Samprati, 7-9, 47n, 116n
Samrāṭ, 45, 47n
Saṁyogitā, 96n
Saṁyutta Nikāya, 77
Sanaq, 103
Sandrokottos (Candragupta), 1, 100, 127-8
Sangala (Saṅkalā), 29
Saṅgha, 71
Saṅghas (oligarchies), 50
Saṅkarṣaṇa, 75, 95n
Sāṅkhya,
philosophy, 100, 109
Sannidhātṛ (chamberlain), 52
Sannyāsin, 84
Sanskrit (language of the elite), 100
Sarasvatī,
river, 26
Sarmanes, 73, 77
Śaśigupta, 27
Śatadhanvan, 8-9
Satrap, 61
Satrapes, 108
Satyavatī, 96n
Saubhuti, 29, 110
Saurāṣṭra,
Surāṣṭra, 39, 61-2, 84
Schwanbeck, 10
Sculpture, 106
Seleucus Nicator,
date and account of the war and treaty of-, with Candragupta, 40-1; 45, 49, 114, 127-8
Senāpati (commander-in-chief), 52, 55

Seven classes of Indian population, 81-4

Shamasastry, R., 11, 69n, 70n

Shatranj (chess), 108

Siboi, 29

Siṁhala, 36

Sindh, 27, 30-2, 37-8, 62

Sindhu (Sindh), 57

Sindhu (Indus),
    river, 27

Śiśunāga, 4-5, 17, 20-1, 23

Śiśunāgadāsa, 20

Śiśunāgas, 4, 12n, 22

Slavery, 87-8

Smith, V.A., 11, 41, 46n, 51, 68n, 106, 108, 116

Somayajñas (sacrifices with oblation of soma juice), 72

Somadeva, 9

Somaśarman, 8

Son,
    river, 42

Sophytes, 29

Sourasenoi, 76

Sparta, 31

Spooner, D.B., 107-8

Śramaṇas, 77-8, 81

Śrauta sūtras, 72, 99

Śrauta Yajñas (sacrifices enjoined by the Śruti or Veda), 72

Sravan Belgola, 44, 78-9

Śrāvastī, 16

Śreṇī(s), 94

Śreṇīmukhyas, 53

Śreṣṭhin, 94

Śreya, 72

Śrīdhara, 46n

Sri Lanka, 1-2, 6, 19, 23

Stadia, 59,
    definition of-, 69n

Stein, O., 11

Sternbach, Ludwik, 110n

Sthaviras, 77

Sthavirāvalīs, 103

Sthūlabhadra, 78

Strabo, 10, 41, 46n, 77, 81-2, 89

Strīdhana, 86-7

Subandhu, 126

Subhadrā, 96n

Sudarśana (lake),
    construction of-,
    by Puṣyagupta, 61
    history of-, 129-31

Śūdra(s), 21, 34, 80-3, 87, 102-3

Sukanyā, 96n

Śuṅgas, 76

Śūrasena, 15, 24, 101

Śūrasenas, 23, 76

Susa, 42, 107, 111n

Susunāga, 7

Suttapiṭaka, 77

Suvarṇagiri, 62

Suvarṇasikatā,
    river, 130

Suyasāḥ, 8

Svapnavāsavadattam, 18, 22

Śvetāmbara (sect of Jains), 95n

Swat,
  river, 26

Syria, 6, 75

Takṣaśilā (Taxila), 27

Tamil,
  language, 40
  land, 50

Tārānātha, 49, 110n

Taxila (Takṣaśilā),
  capital of Āmbhi, 27
  provincial capital of the Maurya empire, 57
  headquarters of the Mauryan viceroy of north-western provinces, 62
  abode of sage Dandamis, 73
  connected with the royal road, 95
  Cāṇakya educated at, 101
  a centre of education and a university town, 104, 108-9

Textile industry, 92

Thomas, F.W., 11, 46n

Tinnevelly, 40

Tīrthaṅkara, 24

Tiṣyarakṣitā, 45n

Tithes on sales,
  board in charge of-, 59

Tod, J., 34

Trade,
  in the Maurya period, 93-4

Tripiṭaka, 77

Turvaśa, 96n

Tuṣāspha,
  Yavana rājā and governor of Aśoka in Surāṣṭra, 50, 2, 131

Udayana, 18-9

Udāyi-baddha, 6

Udāyin, 2-5
  foundation of Pāṭaliputra by, 19; 21, 96n

Ugrasena (epithet of King Nanda), 23, 25

Ujjain, 57,
  capital of the Maurya viceroy of western India, 62
  centre of education, 104

Upanayana, 84

Upaniṣads, 72, 99

Urjayat,
  mountain, 130

Uṣṇīṣa, 96n

Uttarādhyayana sūtra, 35

Uttar Pradesh, 15-6
  eastern, 101
  western, 101

Vadha,
  definition of-, 66, 70n

Vaiśālī, 18, 77

Vaiśeṣika,
philosophy, 100
Vaiśya(s), 61-2, 80, 82-4, 95n
Vājapeya (name of a sacrifice meaning "drink of strength," 72
Vajji, 15-6
Vajjis, Vrajis, 18, 50
Vālmīki, 99
Vanapāla (forest officer), 54, 60
Vānaprastha, 84
Varaṇā (Aornos), 27
Vārāṇasī,
capital of the province of Kāśī, 20
seat of learning, 104
Varṇas, 79
Varṇa-saṅkara, 81
Varuṇa, 72
Vasātis, 30
Vāsavadattā, 18-9, 96n
Vasiṣṭha, 96n
Vāsudeva, 75-6
Vatsa, 15-6, 18, 20, 23-4
Vatsa,
Vātsyāyana (group of the Bhṛgu clan to which Cāṇakya belonged), 101
Vātsyāyana (author of *Kāmasūtra*), 103
Vāyu Purāṇa, 2-4, 7-9
Vedāṅgas, 99-100
Vedānta,
philosophy, 100
Vedas, 99, 105
Vedic religion, 44, 71-2, 75, 109
Vehicles,
in the Maurya period, 95
Viceroys, 61-2
Videha, 101
Vikrama, 2
Vikrama era, 2
Vinayapiṭaka, 77
Vinaya Suttas, 76
Vipāś (Beas),
river, 29
Virūdhaka, Viḍūḍabha, 35, 117
Visākhadatta, 9, 114
Viṣṇu, 75
Viṣṇugupta (personal name of Cāṇakya), 11, 101
Viṣṇu Purāṇa, 8-9, 34, 46n
Vital statistics,
board in charge of-, 58
Vitastā (Jhelum),
river, 27
Vītihotras, 17, 23

War office, 55
Weber, A., 104
Wells, H.G., 115
West Asia,
trade with-, 94

Widows,
remarriage of-, 86
Winternitz, M., 11
Wood work, 93

Xandrammes, 25

Yadu, 96n
Yajñas, 72
Yājñavalkya, 96n
Yājñavalkya Smṛti, 11
Yakṣa(s), 106
Yakṣiṇī, 106
Yamunā,
river, 76
Yaśa, 21
Yāska, 99
Yaśobhadra, 103
Yaugandharāyaṇa, 18-9
Yavan(s) (Ionians), 50, 62, 109, 131
Yavanānī (Greek script), 109
Yoga,
philosophy, 100
Yogananda, 126-7
Yuvarāja (crown prince), 52

Zeus, 73